THE LOGBOOK FOR CYCLISTS

Thunder's Mouth Press

Tour de France cyclists arriving on the Rue de Rivoli; Paris, France, 1980.

THE FITNESS LOGBOOK FOR CYCLISTS

THE ESSENTIAL TRAINING DIARY
FOR CYCLISTS AND TRIATHLETES

INTRODUCTION BY

LIZ BARRETT

THUNDER'S
MOUTH
PRESS

A Balliett & Fitzgerald Book

Book and cover design: Maria Fernandez
Front cover photograph © Jack Popowich

ISBN 1-56025-124-7

First Printing 1997
Printed in the U.S.A.

Published by
Thunder's Mouth Press
632 Broadway, Seventh Floor
New York, NY 10012

Distributed by
Publishers Group West
4065 Hollis Street
Emeryville, CA 94608
(800) 788–3123

A Balliett & Fitzgerald Book
Balliett & Fitzgerald, Inc.
Editorial director: Will Balliett
Production editor: Maria Fernandez
Photo editor: f-stop Fitzgerald
Art director: Sue Canavan
Consulting editor: Liz Barrett
Athletic consultants: Bruce Messite, Louis Gross
Editorial assistants: Aram Song, Ben Welch, Paige Wilder

CONTENTS

Joseph Dundee at Cyclocross; Brockton, Massachusetts.

INTRODUCTION

E very cyclist and triathlete—from world-class competitor to weekend warrior—can go farther and faster with the right training program, an individual plan designed to help achieve goals.

If you are a cyclist, your plan will focus on cycling, but will probably also include other cross-training activities to round out your overall level of fitness. If you are a triathlete, you need a comprehensive plan that emphasizes swimming and running along with cycling, a cross-training regimen that our training logs (see below) are designed to facilitate.

No matter what your plan is, the most important—and often difficult—task is to stick with it. *The Fitness Logbook* will help you do that. It is an indispensable tool for setting goals, recording your workouts, charting your progress, fine-tuning your training program, and giving you a boost just when you need it.

Need a little extra motivation? Open the book to some of your past training notes and see how far you've come in just a short time. You'll see without a doubt that your training is working and you are getting closer to your goals. Got an important race coming up? Check out your notes for similar races you've done in the past. You can see exactly what you did right and hone in on any weak spots that may need extra attention before your next race.

The structure of this book is based on the hardwon wisdom of the best cycling coaches: Take one step at a time, stay focused, and cover all the bases. Start with the year-at-a-glance Training Plan on page four. It will help you set goals and formulate the exact types of training you'll need to reach them. Then use the daily logs to record your workouts and the weekly summaries to track your progress. The fifty-two weekly sections are undated so you can start your year according to your own individual plan. Finally, there are logs for twenty-one touring days and eighteen races. In the back of the book you'll find a metric conversion chart, our editors' selection of important races, tours, triathlons and duathlons, a nation-wide list of cycling resources (useful for finding yet more races), a personal contacts section, and a maintenance calendar.

This book will not tell you how to train, but it will help you stay focused *on* your training so you can meet—or surpass—your goals.

Creating a Training Plan

Every training plan begins with a goal. What do you want to do this year? Do you want to increase your fitness level? Ride a century (a 100 mile race)? Win a triathlon? No matter what you want, you need to identify your goals and write them down.

The Training Plan on page four will help you outline what you want to achieve and what you need to do to get there. It is a year-long template, broken down into four-week "cycles" so you can set short-term as well as long-term goals. Let's say your long-term goal for the year is to increase the distance you are able to ride comfortably from 10 miles to 100 miles. You can meet that goal by adding 10 percent each week. That would be just one extra mile the first week. At the end of the first four-week cycle, you would be riding close to 15 miles, and after the sixth cycle, you would be at or near your goal of 100 miles. Writing that plan down and looking at it on paper will help you set goals that are realistic.

Remember that efficiency, not excess, is the key to a successful training program. You will get the most benefit in the least amount of time by using a combination of approaches—or levels—of training. Level I, "base" training, builds your aerobic capacity with high-volume (i.e. longer duration) and low-intensity workouts at 60 to 70 percent of your maximum heart rate (which should be determined before you begin any exercise or training program). Level II, "intensity" training, is both high-volume and high-intensity, keeping your heart rate at 80 to 90 percent of your maximum with interval training, riding hills, and speed work. Level III, "peak" training, is where you want to be when you race, going full-out, as fast and hard as you can, for short periods of time. Level IV, "active rest," is a brief layoff from serious cycling during which you continue to do moderate exercise, such as light swimming or easy strength training, just to stay in shape. If you are training for a race, you might train at Level 1 for 10 to 12 weeks, Level II for four weeks, Level III for four weeks, and Level IV for one to four weeks.

When you complete your Training Plan form, be sure to note the "focus" for each four-week cycle (aerobic build-up, strength training, interval training, hills, speed work, etc.) and the "activity," or other specific sports, if any, which you will incorporate into your training. This is particularly important for triathletes, who may be training equally as strenuously in swimming and running.

Training Logs

Now to the heart of this book—the daily training logs. Each one-week section begins on Monday and ends on Sunday, with a summary at the end. The daily logs are designed to make it as easy as possible for you to record all the information you need in a simple, at-a-glance format.

The first three entries record the time of day, the actual calendar week, and the week number in your training plan. Then note the route and conditions of the ride. Was it hilly, flat, rocky, hot, humid, cold, icy, high-altitude? This type of information is particularly useful to determine how your performance varies according to particular conditions.

Note both your actual "ride time" (exclusive of stops) and the total time you were out on your bike, as well as the total distance you rode, your average and maximum speed (many speedometers display both), any injuries you already had or suffered during the ride, your weight after the ride, and your average pulse rate during the ride. The pulse record will help you track whether or not you are staying within your targeted heart rate for your training level (base, intensity or peak).

If you did any non-cycling workouts, be sure to enter those as cross-training. Note specific information such as the type of strength training, for example, including the weights, exercises and number of repetitions. Triathletes can use this section to record summaries of all running and swimming workouts as well. This will help give an ongoing overview of total training progress.

The "Comments" section is more important than it may look. Think of it as a diary for future reference. You many want to note how you feel before and after a workout, or an improvement you noticed after adjusting your position on the bike, for example. All of this information will help you fine-tune your training and enhance your performance each week.

Touring Logs

The touring logs may be used as a record of a vacation, or organized tour, or for your own individual treks. The entries are easy-to-use, and will serve as an especially important tool for cyclists who are increasing their mileage toward the goal of a long ride such as a century (100 miles). Make sure to record your average pulse so that you keep it within the appropriate range, and your average speed so that you can make adjustments if necessary.

Racing Logs

When race day comes, you will probably have dozens of things on your mind that seem more pressing than filling out a log form, but be sure to find time to do it anyway. It will show you how your efforts are paying off, and, if you want, help you shoot for even higher goals in the future.

The racing log is designed to be used for all kinds of races, so use it however it suits both your particular needs and the event in which you are competing. For example, in a road race, your job is usually to help your team come out ahead in the end, so your individual time and position may not reflect your ability as a time-trial rider. But if you are riding a time trial, your average speed will be a major factor.

There are some things you should always note, however, such as temperature and conditions. If you have been training at sea level on flat roads, you obviously cannot expect to race as well on a hilly course in high altitude. In that case, you either need to adjust your training or consider different races.

Finally, the most important thing to remember—no matter what kind of cyclist you are or how you plan to use this logbook—is that in the end it is your own progress that really matters. If you finish a race fifth instead of first, don't get stuck on it. Look back at your training logs and see how much faster you can ride now compared to six months ago. If your century turned out to be a 90-miler, turn to Week one and remember when you were lucky to ride 10 miles. Always shoot for more, but never forget to enjoy the sheer pleasure of feeling the wind in your face.

Training Plan for the Year

Training Levels: Level I (Base); Level II (Intensity); Level III (Peak); Level IV (Rest)
Each cycle consists of a 4 week training schedule

Events and competitions: _____

Goal training hours for the year: _____

Cycle	Weeks	Dates	Training Level	Training Focus	Training Activity	Training hours per week — week number				Total hours in cycle
						1	2	3	4	
1										
2										
3										
4										
5										
6										
7										
8										
9										
10										
11										
12										
13										

TRAINING

Raymond Lussier at the Massachusetts Senior Games; 1996.

TRAINING

Monday/Hour:_____ Week of: _____ Week #:_____

Route:_____ Temp./conditions:_____

Ride time: _____ Total time: _____

Distance:_____ Avg. speed: _____ Max. speed:_____

Fitness:_____ Weight: _____ Pulse:_____

Cross-training:_____

Comments:_____

Tuesday/Hour:_____ Week of: _____ Week #:_____

Route:_____ Temp./conditions:_____

Ride time: _____ Total time: _____

Distance:_____ Avg. speed: _____ Max. speed:_____

Fitness:_____ Weight: _____ Pulse:_____

Cross-training:_____

Comments:_____

Wednesday/Hour:_____ Week of: _____ Week #:_____

Route:_____ Temp./conditions:_____

Ride time: _____ Total time: _____

Distance:_____ Avg. speed: _____ Max. speed:_____

Fitness:_____ Weight: _____ Pulse:_____

Cross-training:_____

Comments:_____

Thursday/Hour:_____ Week of: _____ Week #:_____

Route:_____ Temp./conditions:_____

Ride time: _____ Total time: _____

Distance:_____ Avg. speed: _____ Max. speed:_____

Fitness:_____ Weight: _____ Pulse:_____

Cross-training:_____

Comments:_____

Friday/Hour:_____ Week of:_____ Week #:_____

Route:_____ Temp./conditions:_____

Ride time:_____ Total time:_____

Distance:_____ Avg. speed:_____ Max. speed:_____

Fitness:_____ Weight:_____ Pulse:_____

Cross-training:_____

Comments:_____
_____

Saturday/Hour:_____ Week of:_____ Week #:_____

Route:_____ Temp./conditions:_____

Ride time:_____ Total time:_____

Distance:_____ Avg. speed:_____ Max. speed:_____

Fitness:_____ Weight:_____ Pulse:_____

Cross-training:_____

Comments:_____
_____

Sunday/Hour:_____ Week of:_____ Week #:_____

Route:_____ Temp./conditions:_____

Ride time:_____ Total time:_____

Distance:_____ Avg. speed:_____ Max. speed:_____

Fitness:_____ Weight:_____ Pulse:_____

Cross-training:_____

Comments:_____
_____

Weekly Summary

Week of:_____ Week #:_____

Goal hours:_____ Total hours:_____ Goal miles:_____ Total miles:_____

Intensity goal:_____ Avg. speed:_____ Max. speed:_____

Fitness:_____ Weight:_____ Pulse:_____

Other training goals:_____

Cross-training:_____

Equipment/Maintenance:_____

Comments:_____
_____

Monday/Hour:_____ Week of:_____ Week #:_____

Route:_____ Temp./conditions:_____

Ride time:_____ Total time:_____

Distance:_____ Avg. speed:_____ Max. speed:_____

Fitness:_____ Weight:_____ Pulse:_____

Cross-training:_____

Comments:_____

Tuesday/Hour:_____ Week of:_____ Week #:_____

Route:_____ Temp./conditions:_____

Ride time:_____ Total time:_____

Distance:_____ Avg. speed:_____ Max. speed:_____

Fitness:_____ Weight:_____ Pulse:_____

Cross-training:_____

Comments:_____

Wednesday/Hour:_____ Week of:_____ Week #:_____

Route:_____ Temp./conditions:_____

Ride time:_____ Total time:_____

Distance:_____ Avg. speed:_____ Max. speed:_____

Fitness:_____ Weight:_____ Pulse:_____

Cross-training:_____

Comments:_____

Thursday/Hour:_____ Week of:_____ Week #:_____

Route:_____ Temp./conditions:_____

Ride time:_____ Total time:_____

Distance:_____ Avg. speed:_____ Max. speed:_____

Fitness:_____ Weight:_____ Pulse:_____

Cross-training:_____

Comments:_____

Friday/Hour: _____ Week of: _____ Week #: _____

Route: _____ Temp./conditions: _____

Ride time: _____ Total time: _____

Distance: _____ Avg. speed: _____ Max. speed: _____

Fitness: _____ Weight: _____ Pulse: _____

Cross-training: _____

Comments: _____
_____

Saturday/Hour: _____ Week of: _____ Week #: _____

Route: _____ Temp./conditions: _____

Ride time: _____ Total time: _____

Distance: _____ Avg. speed: _____ Max. speed: _____

Fitness: _____ Weight: _____ Pulse: _____

Cross-training: _____

Comments: _____
_____

Sunday/Hour: _____ Week of: _____ Week #: _____

Route: _____ Temp./conditions: _____

Ride time: _____ Total time: _____

Distance: _____ Avg. speed: _____ Max. speed: _____

Fitness: _____ Weight: _____ Pulse: _____

Cross-training: _____

Comments: _____
_____

Weekly Summary

Week of: _____ Week #: _____

Goal hours: _____ Total hours: _____ Goal miles: _____ Total miles: _____

Intensity goal: _____ Avg. speed: _____ Max. speed: _____

Fitness: _____ Weight: _____ Pulse: _____

Other training goals: _____

Cross-training: _____

Equipment/Maintenance: _____

Comments: _____
_____

Monday/Hour:_____ Week of: _____ Week #:_____

Route:_____ Temp./conditions:_____

Ride time:_____ Total time: _____

Distance:_____ Avg. speed: _____ Max. speed:_____

Fitness:_____ Weight: _____ Pulse:_____

Cross-training:_____

Comments:_____

Tuesday/Hour:_____ Week of: _____ Week #:_____

Route:_____ Temp./conditions:_____

Ride time:_____ Total time: _____

Distance:_____ Avg. speed: _____ Max. speed:_____

Fitness:_____ Weight: _____ Pulse:_____

Cross-training:_____

Comments:_____

Wednesday/Hour:_____ Week of: _____ Week #:_____

Route:_____ Temp./conditions:_____

Ride time:_____ Total time: _____

Distance:_____ Avg. speed: _____ Max. speed:_____

Fitness:_____ Weight: _____ Pulse:_____

Cross-training:_____

Comments:_____

Thursday/Hour:_____ Week of: _____ Week #:_____

Route:_____ Temp./conditions:_____

Ride time:_____ Total time: _____

Distance:_____ Avg. speed: _____ Max. speed:_____

Fitness:_____ Weight: _____ Pulse:_____

Cross-training:_____

Comments:_____

Friday/Hour:_____ Week of:_____ Week #:_____

Route:_____ Temp./conditions:_____

Ride time:_____ Total time:_____

Distance:_____ Avg. speed:_____ Max. speed:_____

Fitness:_____ Weight:_____ Pulse:_____

Cross-training:_____

_____

Comments:_____

_____

Saturday/Hour:_____ Week of:_____ Week #:_____

Route:_____ Temp./conditions:_____

Ride time:_____ Total time:_____

Distance:_____ Avg. speed:_____ Max. speed:_____

Fitness:_____ Weight:_____ Pulse:_____

Cross-training:_____

Comments:_____

_____

Sunday/Hour:_____ Week of:_____ Week #:_____

Route:_____ Temp./conditions:_____

Ride time:_____ Total time:_____

Distance:_____ Avg. speed:_____ Max. speed:_____

Fitness:_____ Weight:_____ Pulse:_____

Cross-training:_____

_____

Comments:_____

_____

Weekly Summary

Week of:_____ Week #:_____

Goal hours:_____ Total hours:_____ Goal miles:_____ Total miles:_____

Intensity goal:_____ Avg. speed:_____ Max. speed:_____

Fitness:_____ Weight:_____ Pulse:_____

Other training goals:_____

Cross-training:_____

Equipment/Maintenance:_____

Comments:_____

_____

Monday/Hour:_____ Week of: _____ Week #:_____

Route:_____ Temp./conditions:_____

Ride time:_____ Total time: _____

Distance:_____ Avg. speed: _____ Max. speed:_____

Fitness:_____ Weight: _____ Pulse:_____

Cross-training:_____

_____

Comments:_____

_____

_____

Tuesday/Hour:_____ Week of: _____ Week #:_____

Route:_____ Temp./conditions:_____

Ride time:_____ Total time: _____

Distance:_____ Avg. speed: _____ Max. speed:_____

Fitness:_____ Weight: _____ Pulse:_____

Cross-training:_____

_____

Comments:_____

_____

Wednesday/Hour:_____ Week of: _____ Week #:_____

Route:_____ Temp./conditions:_____

Ride time:_____ Total time: _____

Distance:_____ Avg. speed: _____ Max. speed:_____

Fitness:_____ Weight: _____ Pulse:_____

Cross-training:_____

_____

Comments:_____

_____

_____

Thursday/Hour:_____ Week of: _____ Week #:_____

Route:_____ Temp./conditions:_____

Ride time:_____ Total time: _____

Distance:_____ Avg. speed: _____ Max. speed:_____

Fitness:_____ Weight: _____ Pulse:_____

Cross-training:_____

_____

Comments:_____

_____

Friday/Hour:_____ Week of:_____ Week #:_____

Route:_____ Temp./conditions:_____

Ride time:_____ Total time:_____

Distance:_____ Avg. speed:_____ Max. speed:_____

Fitness:_____ Weight:_____ Pulse:_____

Cross-training:_____

_____

Comments:_____

_____

Saturday/Hour:_____ Week of:_____ Week #:_____

Route:_____ Temp./conditions:_____

Ride time:_____ Total time:_____

Distance:_____ Avg. speed:_____ Max. speed:_____

Fitness:_____ Weight:_____ Pulse:_____

Cross-training:_____

_____

Comments:_____

_____

Sunday/Hour:_____ Week of:_____ Week #:_____

Route:_____ Temp./conditions:_____

Ride time:_____ Total time:_____

Distance:_____ Avg. speed:_____ Max. speed:_____

Fitness:_____ Weight:_____ Pulse:_____

Cross-training:_____

_____

Comments:_____

_____

Weekly Summary

Week of:_____ Week #:_____

Goal hours:_____ Total hours:_____ Goal miles:_____ Total miles:_____

Intensity goal:_____ Avg. speed:_____ Max. speed:_____

Fitness:_____ Weight:_____ Pulse:_____

Other training goals:_____

Cross-training:_____

Equipment/Maintenance:_____

Comments:_____

_____

Racers spin around in a sharp curve on the wooden track in the International Six-Day Bike Race.

TRAINING

Monday/Hour:_____ Week of:_____ Week #:_____

Route:_____ Temp./conditions:_____

Ride time:_____ Total time:_____

Distance:_____ Avg. speed:_____ Max. speed:_____

Fitness:_____ Weight:_____ Pulse:_____

Cross-training:_____

Comments:_____

Tuesday/Hour:_____ Week of:_____ Week #:_____

Route:_____ Temp./conditions:_____

Ride time:_____ Total time:_____

Distance:_____ Avg. speed:_____ Max. speed:_____

Fitness:_____ Weight:_____ Pulse:_____

Cross-training:_____

Comments:_____

Wednesday/Hour:_____ Week of:_____ Week #:_____

Route:_____ Temp./conditions:_____

Ride time:_____ Total time:_____

Distance:_____ Avg. speed:_____ Max. speed:_____

Fitness:_____ Weight:_____ Pulse:_____

Cross-training:_____

Comments:_____

Thursday/Hour:_____ Week of:_____ Week #:_____

Route:_____ Temp./conditions:_____

Ride time:_____ Total time:_____

Distance:_____ Avg. speed:_____ Max. speed:_____

Fitness:_____ Weight:_____ Pulse:_____

Cross-training:_____

Comments:_____

Friday/Hour:_____ Week of:_____ Week #:_____

Route:_____ Temp./conditions:_____

Ride time:_____ Total time:_____

Distance:_____ Avg. speed:_____ Max. speed:_____

Fitness:_____ Weight:_____ Pulse:_____

Cross-training:_____

Comments:_____
_____

Saturday/Hour:_____ Week of:_____ Week #:_____

Route:_____ Temp./conditions:_____

Ride time:_____ Total time:_____

Distance:_____ Avg. speed:_____ Max. speed:_____

Fitness:_____ Weight:_____ Pulse:_____

Cross-training:_____

Comments:_____
_____

Sunday/Hour:_____ Week of:_____ Week #:_____

Route:_____ Temp./conditions:_____

Ride time:_____ Total time:_____

Distance:_____ Avg. speed:_____ Max. speed:_____

Fitness:_____ Weight:_____ Pulse:_____

Cross-training:_____

Comments:_____
_____

Weekly Summary

Week of:_____ Week #:_____

Goal hours:_____ Total hours:_____ Goal miles:_____ Total miles:_____

Intensity goal:_____ Avg. speed:_____ Max. speed:_____

Fitness:_____ Weight:_____ Pulse:_____

Other training goals:_____

Cross-training:_____

Equipment/Maintenance:_____

Comments:_____
_____

TRAINING

Monday/Hour:_____ Week of:_____ Week #:_____

Route:_____ Temp./conditions:_____

Ride time:_____ Total time:_____

Distance:_____ Avg. speed:_____ Max. speed:_____

Fitness:_____ Weight:_____ Pulse:_____

Cross-training:_____

Comments:_____

Tuesday/Hour:_____ Week of:_____ Week #:_____

Route:_____ Temp./conditions:_____

Ride time:_____ Total time:_____

Distance:_____ Avg. speed:_____ Max. speed:_____

Fitness:_____ Weight:_____ Pulse:_____

Cross-training:_____

Comments:_____

Wednesday/Hour:_____ Week of:_____ Week #:_____

Route:_____ Temp./conditions:_____

Ride time:_____ Total time:_____

Distance:_____ Avg. speed:_____ Max. speed:_____

Fitness:_____ Weight:_____ Pulse:_____

Cross-training:_____

Comments:_____

Thursday/Hour:_____ Week of:_____ Week #:_____

Route:_____ Temp./conditions:_____

Ride time:_____ Total time:_____

Distance:_____ Avg. speed:_____ Max. speed:_____

Fitness:_____ Weight:_____ Pulse:_____

Cross-training:_____

Comments:_____

Friday/Hour:_____ Week of:_____ Week #:_____

Route:_____ Temp./conditions:_____

Ride time:_____ Total time:_____

Distance:_____ Avg. speed:_____ Max. speed:_____

Fitness:_____ Weight:_____ Pulse:_____

Cross-training:_____

Comments:_____

Saturday/Hour:_____ Week of:_____ Week #:_____

Route:_____ Temp./conditions:_____

Ride time:_____ Total time:_____

Distance:_____ Avg. speed:_____ Max. speed:_____

Fitness:_____ Weight:_____ Pulse:_____

Cross-training:_____

Comments:_____

Sunday/Hour:_____ Week of:_____ Week #:_____

Route:_____ Temp./conditions:_____

Ride time:_____ Total time:_____

Distance:_____ Avg. speed:_____ Max. speed:_____

Fitness:_____ Weight:_____ Pulse:_____

Cross-training:_____

Comments:_____

Weekly Summary

Week of:_____ Week #:_____

Goal hours:_____ Total hours:_____ Goal miles:_____ Total miles:_____

Intensity goal:_____ Avg. speed:_____ Max. speed:_____

Fitness:_____ Weight:_____ Pulse:_____

Other training goals:_____

Cross-training:_____

Equipment/Maintenance:_____

Comments:_____

Monday/Hour:_____ Week of:_____ Week #:_____

Route:_____ Temp./conditions:_____

Ride time:_____ Total time:_____

Distance:_____ Avg. speed:_____ Max. speed:_____

Fitness:_____ Weight:_____ Pulse:_____

Cross-training:_____

Comments:_____

Tuesday/Hour:_____ Week of:_____ Week #:_____

Route:_____ Temp./conditions:_____

Ride time:_____ Total time:_____

Distance:_____ Avg. speed:_____ Max. speed:_____

Fitness:_____ Weight:_____ Pulse:_____

Cross-training:_____

Comments:_____

Wednesday/Hour:_____ Week of:_____ Week #:_____

Route:_____ Temp./conditions:_____

Ride time:_____ Total time:_____

Distance:_____ Avg. speed:_____ Max. speed:_____

Fitness:_____ Weight:_____ Pulse:_____

Cross-training:_____

Comments:_____

Thursday/Hour:_____ Week of:_____ Week #:_____

Route:_____ Temp./conditions:_____

Ride time:_____ Total time:_____

Distance:_____ Avg. speed:_____ Max. speed:_____

Fitness:_____ Weight:_____ Pulse:_____

Cross-training:_____

Comments:_____

TRAINING

Friday/Hour:_____ Week of:_____ Week #:_____

Route:_____ Temp./conditions:_____

Ride time:_____ Total time:_____

Distance:_____ Avg. speed:_____ Max. speed:_____

Fitness:_____ Weight:_____ Pulse:_____

Cross-training:_____

Comments:_____
_____

Saturday/Hour:_____ Week of:_____ Week #:_____

Route:_____ Temp./conditions:_____

Ride time:_____ Total time:_____

Distance:_____ Avg. speed:_____ Max. speed:_____

Fitness:_____ Weight:_____ Pulse:_____

Cross-training:_____

Comments:_____
_____

Sunday/Hour:_____ Week of:_____ Week #:_____

Route:_____ Temp./conditions:_____

Ride time:_____ Total time:_____

Distance:_____ Avg. speed:_____ Max. speed:_____

Fitness:_____ Weight:_____ Pulse:_____

Cross-training:_____

Comments:_____
_____

Weekly Summary

Week of:_____ Week #:_____

Goal hours:_____ Total hours:_____ Goal miles:_____ Total miles:_____

Intensity goal:_____ Avg. speed:_____ Max. speed:_____

Fitness:_____ Weight:_____ Pulse:_____

Other training goals:_____

Cross-training:_____

Equipment/Maintenance:_____

Comments:_____
_____

20

Monday/Hour:_____ Week of: _____ Week #:_____

Route:_____ Temp./conditions:_____

Ride time:_____ Total time: _____

Distance:_____ Avg. speed: _____ Max. speed:_____

Fitness:_____ Weight: _____ Pulse:_____

Cross-training:_____

_____

Comments:_____

_____

Tuesday/Hour:_____ Week of: _____ Week #:_____

Route:_____ Temp./conditions:_____

Ride time:_____ Total time: _____

Distance:_____ Avg. speed: _____ Max. speed:_____

Fitness:_____ Weight: _____ Pulse:_____

Cross-training:_____

_____

Comments:_____

_____

Wednesday/Hour:_____ Week of: _____ Week #:_____

Route:_____ Temp./conditions:_____

Ride time:_____ Total time: _____

Distance:_____ Avg. speed: _____ Max. speed:_____

Fitness:_____ Weight: _____ Pulse:_____

Cross-training:_____

_____

Comments:_____

_____

Thursday/Hour:_____ Week of: _____ Week #:_____

Route:_____ Temp./conditions:_____

Ride time:_____ Total time: _____

Distance:_____ Avg. speed: _____ Max. speed:_____

Fitness:_____ Weight: _____ Pulse:_____

Cross-training:_____

_____

Comments:_____

_____

21

Friday/Hour:_____ Week of:_____ Week #:_____

Route:_____ Temp./conditions:_____

Ride time:_____ Total time:_____

Distance:_____ Avg. speed:_____ Max. speed:_____

Fitness:_____ Weight:_____ Pulse:_____

Cross-training:_____

_____

Comments:_____

_____

Saturday/Hour:_____ Week of:_____ Week #:_____

Route:_____ Temp./conditions:_____

Ride time:_____ Total time:_____

Distance:_____ Avg. speed:_____ Max. speed:_____

Fitness:_____ Weight:_____ Pulse:_____

Cross-training:_____

_____

Comments:_____

_____

Sunday/Hour:_____ Week of:_____ Week #:_____

Route:_____ Temp./conditions:_____

Ride time:_____ Total time:_____

Distance:_____ Avg. speed:_____ Max. speed:_____

Fitness:_____ Weight:_____ Pulse:_____

Cross-training:_____

_____

Comments:_____

_____

Weekly Summary

Week of:_____ Week #:_____

Goal hours:_____ Total hours:_____ Goal miles:_____ Total miles:_____

Intensity goal:_____ Avg. speed:_____ Max. speed:_____

Fitness:_____ Weight:_____ Pulse:_____

Other training goals:_____

Cross-training:_____

Equipment/Maintenance:_____

Comments:_____

_____

Bike racing between the wars; Newark, New Jersey.

Monday/Hour:_____ Week of:_____ Week #:_____

Route:_____ Temp./conditions:_____

Ride time:_____ Total time:_____

Distance:_____ Avg. speed:_____ Max. speed:_____

Fitness:_____ Weight:_____ Pulse:_____

Cross-training:_____

_____

Comments:_____

_____

Tuesday/Hour:_____ Week of:_____ Week #:_____

Route:_____ Temp./conditions:_____

Ride time:_____ Total time:_____

Distance:_____ Avg. speed:_____ Max. speed:_____

Fitness:_____ Weight:_____ Pulse:_____

Cross-training:_____

_____

Comments:_____

_____

Wednesday/Hour:_____ Week of:_____ Week #:_____

Route:_____ Temp./conditions:_____

Ride time:_____ Total time:_____

Distance:_____ Avg. speed:_____ Max. speed:_____

Fitness:_____ Weight:_____ Pulse:_____

Cross-training:_____

_____

Comments:_____

_____

Thursday/Hour:_____ Week of:_____ Week #:_____

Route:_____ Temp./conditions:_____

Ride time:_____ Total time:_____

Distance:_____ Avg. speed:_____ Max. speed:_____

Fitness:_____ Weight:_____ Pulse:_____

Cross-training:_____

_____

Comments:_____

_____

TRAINING

Friday/Hour: _____ Week of: _____ Week #: _____

Route: _____ Temp./conditions: _____

Ride time: _____ Total time: _____

Distance: _____ Avg. speed: _____ Max. speed: _____

Fitness: _____ Weight: _____ Pulse: _____

Cross-training: _____

Comments: _____

Saturday/Hour: _____ Week of: _____ Week #: _____

Route: _____ Temp./conditions: _____

Ride time: _____ Total time: _____

Distance: _____ Avg. speed: _____ Max. speed: _____

Fitness: _____ Weight: _____ Pulse: _____

Cross-training: _____

Comments: _____

Sunday/Hour: _____ Week of: _____ Week #: _____

Route: _____ Temp./conditions: _____

Ride time: _____ Total time: _____

Distance: _____ Avg. speed: _____ Max. speed: _____

Fitness: _____ Weight: _____ Pulse: _____

Cross-training: _____

Comments: _____

Weekly Summary

Week of: _____ Week #: _____

Goal hours: _____ Total hours: _____ Goal miles: _____ Total miles: _____

Intensity goal: _____ Avg. speed: _____ Max. speed: _____

Fitness: _____ Weight: _____ Pulse: _____

Other training goals: _____

Cross-training: _____

Equipment/Maintenance: _____

Comments: _____

Monday/Hour:_____ Week of: _____ Week #:_____

Route:_____ Temp./conditions:_____

Ride time:_____ Total time: _____

Distance:_____ Avg. speed: _____ Max. speed:_____

Fitness:_____ Weight: _____ Pulse:_____

Cross-training:_____

_____

Comments:_____

_____

Tuesday/Hour:_____ Week of: _____ Week #:_____

Route:_____ Temp./conditions:_____

Ride time:_____ Total time: _____

Distance:_____ Avg. speed: _____ Max. speed:_____

Fitness:_____ Weight: _____ Pulse:_____

Cross-training:_____

_____

Comments:_____

_____

Wednesday/Hour:_____ Week of: _____ Week #:_____

Route:_____ Temp./conditions:_____

Ride time:_____ Total time: _____

Distance:_____ Avg. speed: _____ Max. speed:_____

Fitness:_____ Weight: _____ Pulse:_____

Cross-training:_____

_____

Comments:_____

_____

Thursday/Hour:_____ Week of: _____ Week #:_____

Route:_____ Temp./conditions:_____

Ride time:_____ Total time: _____

Distance:_____ Avg. speed: _____ Max. speed:_____

Fitness:_____ Weight: _____ Pulse:_____

Cross-training:_____

_____

Comments:_____

_____

Friday/Hour:_____ Week of: _____ Week #:_____

Route:_____ Temp./conditions:_____

Ride time:_____ Total time: _____

Distance:_____ Avg. speed: _____ Max. speed:_____

Fitness:_____ Weight: _____ Pulse:_____

Cross-training:_____

_____

Comments:_____

_____

Saturday/Hour:_____ Week of: _____ Week #:_____

Route:_____ Temp./conditions:_____

Ride time:_____ Total time: _____

Distance:_____ Avg. speed: _____ Max. speed:_____

Fitness:_____ Weight: _____ Pulse:_____

Cross-training:_____

_____

Comments:_____

_____

Sunday/Hour:_____ Week of: _____ Week #:_____

Route:_____ Temp./conditions:_____

Ride time:_____ Total time: _____

Distance:_____ Avg. speed: _____ Max. speed:_____

Fitness:_____ Weight: _____ Pulse:_____

Cross-training:_____

_____

Comments:_____

_____

Weekly Summary

Week of:_____ Week #:_____

Goal hours:_____ Total hours:_____ Goal miles:_____ Total miles:_____

Intensity goal:_____ Avg. speed:_____ Max. speed:_____

Fitness:_____ Weight:_____ Pulse:_____

Other training goals:_____

Cross-training:_____

Equipment/Maintenance:_____

Comments:_____

_____

Monday/Hour:_____ Week of:_____ Week #:_____

Route:_____ Temp./conditions:_____

Ride time:_____ Total time:_____

Distance:_____ Avg. speed:_____ Max. speed:_____

Fitness:_____ Weight:_____ Pulse:_____

Cross-training:_____

Comments:_____

Tuesday/Hour:_____ Week of:_____ Week #:_____

Route:_____ Temp./conditions:_____

Ride time:_____ Total time:_____

Distance:_____ Avg. speed:_____ Max. speed:_____

Fitness:_____ Weight:_____ Pulse:_____

Cross-training:_____

Comments:_____

Wednesday/Hour:_____ Week of:_____ Week #:_____

Route:_____ Temp./conditions:_____

Ride time:_____ Total time:_____

Distance:_____ Avg. speed:_____ Max. speed:_____

Fitness:_____ Weight:_____ Pulse:_____

Cross-training:_____

Comments:_____

Thursday/Hour:_____ Week of:_____ Week #:_____

Route:_____ Temp./conditions:_____

Ride time:_____ Total time:_____

Distance:_____ Avg. speed:_____ Max. speed:_____

Fitness:_____ Weight:_____ Pulse:_____

Cross-training:_____

Comments:_____

Friday/Hour:_____ Week of:_____ Week #:_____

Route:_____ Temp./conditions:_____

Ride time:_____ Total time:_____

Distance:_____ Avg. speed:_____ Max. speed:_____

Fitness:_____ Weight:_____ Pulse:_____

Cross-training:_____

Comments:_____

Saturday/Hour:_____ Week of:_____ Week #:_____

Route:_____ Temp./conditions:_____

Ride time:_____ Total time:_____

Distance:_____ Avg. speed:_____ Max. speed:_____

Fitness:_____ Weight:_____ Pulse:_____

Cross-training:_____

Comments:_____

Sunday/Hour:_____ Week of:_____ Week #:_____

Route:_____ Temp./conditions:_____

Ride time:_____ Total time:_____

Distance:_____ Avg. speed:_____ Max. speed:_____

Fitness:_____ Weight:_____ Pulse:_____

Cross-training:_____

Comments:_____

Weekly Summary

Week of:_____ Week #:_____

Goal hours:_____ Total hours:_____ Goal miles:_____ Total miles:_____

Intensity goal:_____ Avg. speed:_____ Max. speed:_____

Fitness:_____ Weight:_____ Pulse:_____

Other training goals:_____

Cross-training:_____

Equipment/Maintenance:_____

Comments:_____

TRAINING

TRAINING

Monday/Hour:_____ Week of:_____ Week #:_____

Route:_____ Temp./conditions:_____

Ride time:_____ Total time:_____

Distance:_____ Avg. speed:_____ Max. speed:_____

Fitness:_____ Weight:_____ Pulse:_____

Cross-training:_____

_____

Comments:_____

_____

Tuesday/Hour:_____ Week of:_____ Week #:_____

Route:_____ Temp./conditions:_____

Ride time:_____ Total time:_____

Distance:_____ Avg. speed:_____ Max. speed:_____

Fitness:_____ Weight:_____ Pulse:_____

Cross-training:_____

_____

Comments:_____

_____

Wednesday/Hour:_____ Week of:_____ Week #:_____

Route:_____ Temp./conditions:_____

Ride time:_____ Total time:_____

Distance:_____ Avg. speed:_____ Max. speed:_____

Fitness:_____ Weight:_____ Pulse:_____

Cross-training:_____

_____

Comments:_____

_____

Thursday/Hour:_____ Week of:_____ Week #:_____

Route:_____ Temp./conditions:_____

Ride time:_____ Total time:_____

Distance:_____ Avg. speed:_____ Max. speed:_____

Fitness:_____ Weight:_____ Pulse:_____

Cross-training:_____

_____

Comments:_____

_____

Friday/Hour: _____ Week of: _____ Week #: _____

Route: _____ Temp./conditions: _____

Ride time: _____ Total time: _____

Distance: _____ Avg. speed: _____ Max. speed: _____

Fitness: _____ Weight: _____ Pulse: _____

Cross-training: _____

_____

Comments: _____

_____

Saturday/Hour: _____ Week of: _____ Week #: _____

Route: _____ Temp./conditions: _____

Ride time: _____ Total time: _____

Distance: _____ Avg. speed: _____ Max. speed: _____

Fitness: _____ Weight: _____ Pulse: _____

Cross-training: _____

_____

Comments: _____

_____

Sunday/Hour: _____ Week of: _____ Week #: _____

Route: _____ Temp./conditions: _____

Ride time: _____ Total time: _____

Distance: _____ Avg. speed: _____ Max. speed: _____

Fitness: _____ Weight: _____ Pulse: _____

Cross-training: _____

_____

Comments: _____

_____

Weekly Summary

Week of: _____ Week #: _____

Goal hours: _____ Total hours: _____ Goal miles: _____ Total miles: _____

Intensity goal: _____ Avg. speed: _____ Max. speed: _____

Fitness: _____ Weight: _____ Pulse: _____

Other training goals: _____

Cross-training: _____

Equipment/Maintenance: _____

Comments: _____

_____

Frank McCormack at the Fitchburg Longsjo Classic; Fitchburg, Massachusetts; 1996.

Monday/Hour:_____ Week of: _____ Week #:_____

Route:_____ Temp./conditions:_____

Ride time:_____ Total time: _____

Distance:_____ Avg. speed: _____ Max. speed:_____

Fitness:_____ Weight: _____ Pulse:_____

Cross-training:_____

Comments:_____
_____

Tuesday/Hour:_____ Week of: _____ Week #:_____

Route:_____ Temp./conditions:_____

Ride time:_____ Total time: _____

Distance:_____ Avg. speed: _____ Max. speed:_____

Fitness:_____ Weight: _____ Pulse:_____

Cross-training:_____

Comments:_____
_____

Wednesday/Hour:_____ Week of: _____ Week #:_____

Route:_____ Temp./conditions:_____

Ride time:_____ Total time: _____

Distance:_____ Avg. speed: _____ Max. speed:_____

Fitness:_____ Weight: _____ Pulse:_____

Cross-training:_____

Comments:_____
_____

Thursday/Hour:_____ Week of: _____ Week #:_____

Route:_____ Temp./conditions:_____

Ride time:_____ Total time: _____

Distance:_____ Avg. speed: _____ Max. speed:_____

Fitness:_____ Weight: _____ Pulse:_____

Cross-training:_____

Comments:_____
_____

Friday/Hour:_____   Week of:_____   Week #:_____

Route:_____   Temp./conditions:_____

Ride time:_____   Total time:_____

Distance:_____   Avg. speed:_____   Max. speed:_____

Fitness:_____   Weight:_____   Pulse:_____

Cross-training:_____

_____

Comments:_____

_____

Saturday/Hour:_____   Week of:_____   Week #:_____

Route:_____   Temp./conditions:_____

Ride time:_____   Total time:_____

Distance:_____   Avg. speed:_____   Max. speed:_____

Fitness:_____   Weight:_____   Pulse:_____

Cross-training:_____

_____

Comments:_____

_____

Sunday/Hour:_____   Week of:_____   Week #:_____

Route:_____   Temp./conditions:_____

Ride time:_____   Total time:_____

Distance:_____   Avg. speed:_____   Max. speed:_____

Fitness:_____   Weight:_____   Pulse:_____

Cross-training:_____

_____

Comments:_____

_____

Weekly Summary

Week of:_____   Week #:_____

Goal hours:_____   Total hours:_____   Goal miles:_____   Total miles:_____

Intensity goal:_____   Avg. speed:_____   Max. speed:_____

Fitness:_____   Weight:_____   Pulse:_____

Other training goals:_____

Cross-training:_____

Equipment/Maintenance:_____

Comments:_____

_____

Monday/Hour:_____ Week of: _____ Week #:_____

Route:_____ Temp./conditions:_____

Ride time:_____ Total time: _____

Distance:_____ Avg. speed: _____ Max. speed:_____

Fitness:_____ Weight: _____ Pulse:_____

Cross-training:_____

_____

Comments:_____

_____

Tuesday/Hour:_____ Week of: _____ Week #:_____

Route:_____ Temp./conditions:_____

Ride time:_____ Total time: _____

Distance:_____ Avg. speed: _____ Max. speed:_____

Fitness:_____ Weight: _____ Pulse:_____

Cross-training:_____

_____

Comments:_____

_____

Wednesday/Hour:_____ Week of: _____ Week #:_____

Route:_____ Temp./conditions:_____

Ride time:_____ Total time: _____

Distance:_____ Avg. speed: _____ Max. speed:_____

Fitness:_____ Weight: _____ Pulse:_____

Cross-training:_____

_____

Comments:_____

_____

Thursday/Hour:_____ Week of: _____ Week #:_____

Route:_____ Temp./conditions:_____

Ride time:_____ Total time: _____

Distance:_____ Avg. speed: _____ Max. speed:_____

Fitness:_____ Weight: _____ Pulse:_____

Cross-training:_____

_____

Comments:_____

_____

TRAINING

Friday/Hour:_____ Week of:_____ Week #:_____
Route:_____ Temp./conditions:_____
Ride time:_____ Total time:_____
Distance:_____ Avg. speed:_____ Max. speed:_____
Fitness:_____ Weight: __,_____ Pulse:_____
Cross-training:_____
_____
Comments:_____
_____

Saturday/Hour:_____ Week of:_____ Week #:_____
Route:_____ Temp./conditions:_____
Ride time:_____ Total time:_____
Distance:_____ Avg. speed:_____ Max. speed:_____
Fitness:_____ Weight:_____ Pulse:_____
Cross-training:_____
_____
Comments:_____
_____

Sunday/Hour:_____ Week of:_____ Week #:_____
Route:_____ Temp./conditions:_____
Ride time:_____ Total time:_____
Distance:_____ Avg. speed:_____ Max. speed:_____
Fitness:_____ Weight:_____ Pulse:_____
Cross-training:_____
_____
Comments:_____
_____

Weekly Summary
Week of:_____ Week #:_____
Goal hours:_____ Total hours:_____ Goal miles:_____ Total miles:_____
Intensity goal:_____ Avg. speed:_____ Max. speed:_____
Fitness:_____ Weight:_____ Pulse:_____
Other training goals:_____
Cross-training:_____
Equipment/Maintenance:_____
Comments:_____
_____

Monday/Hour:_____ Week of:_____ Week #:_____

Route:_____ Temp./conditions:_____

Ride time:_____ Total time:_____

Distance:_____ Avg. speed:_____ Max. speed:_____

Fitness:_____ Weight:_____ Pulse:_____

Cross-training:_____

_____

Comments:_____

_____

Tuesday/Hour:_____ Week of:_____ Week #:_____

Route:_____ Temp./conditions:_____

Ride time:_____ Total time:_____

Distance:_____ Avg. speed:_____ Max. speed:_____

Fitness:_____ Weight:_____ Pulse:_____

Cross-training:_____

Comments:_____

Wednesday/Hour:_____ Week of:_____ Week #:_____

Route:_____ Temp./conditions:_____

Ride time:_____ Total time:_____

Distance:_____ Avg. speed:_____ Max. speed:_____

Fitness:_____ Weight:_____ Pulse:_____

Cross-training:_____

_____

Comments:_____

Thursday/Hour:_____ Week of:_____ Week #:_____

Route:_____ Temp./conditions:_____

Ride time:_____ Total time:_____

Distance:_____ Avg. speed:_____ Max. speed:_____

Fitness:_____ Weight:_____ Pulse:_____

Cross-training:_____

Comments:_____

Friday/Hour:_____ Week of: _____ Week #:_____

Route:_____ Temp./conditions:_____

Ride time: _____ Total time: _____

Distance:_____ Avg. speed: _____ Max. speed:_____

Fitness:_____ Weight: _____ Pulse:_____

Cross-training:_____

Comments:_____

Saturday/Hour:_____ Week of: _____ Week #:_____

Route:_____ Temp./conditions:_____

Ride time: _____ Total time: _____

Distance:_____ Avg. speed: _____ Max. speed:_____

Fitness:_____ Weight: _____ Pulse:_____

Cross-training:_____

Comments:_____

Sunday/Hour:_____ Week of: _____ Week #:_____

Route:_____ Temp./conditions:_____

Ride time: _____ Total time: _____

Distance:_____ Avg. speed: _____ Max. speed:_____

Fitness:_____ Weight: _____ Pulse:_____

Cross-training:_____

Comments:_____

Weekly Summary

Week of:_____ Week #:_____

Goal hours:_____ Total hours:_____ Goal miles: _____ Total miles:_____

Intensity goal: _____ Avg. speed: _____ Max. speed:_____

Fitness:_____ Weight: _____ Pulse:_____

Other training goals:_____

Cross-training: _____

Equipment/Maintenance:_____

Comments:_____

TRAINING

Monday/Hour:_____ Week of:_____ Week #:_____
Route:_____ Temp./conditions:_____
Ride time:_____ Total time:_____
Distance:_____ Avg. speed:_____ Max. speed:_____
Fitness:_____ Weight:_____ Pulse:_____
Cross-training:_____
_____
Comments:_____
_____

Tuesday/Hour:_____ Week of:_____ Week #:_____
Route:_____ Temp./conditions:_____
Ride time:_____ Total time:_____
Distance:_____ Avg. speed:_____ Max. speed:_____
Fitness:_____ Weight:_____ Pulse:_____
Cross-training:_____
_____
Comments:_____
_____

Wednesday/Hour:_____ Week of:_____ Week #:_____
Route:_____ Temp./conditions:_____
Ride time:_____ Total time:_____
Distance:_____ Avg. speed:_____ Max. speed:_____
Fitness:_____ Weight:_____ Pulse:_____
Cross-training:_____
_____
Comments:_____
_____

Thursday/Hour:_____ Week of:_____ Week #:_____
Route:_____ Temp./conditions:_____
Ride time:_____ Total time:_____
Distance:_____ Avg. speed:_____ Max. speed:_____
Fitness:_____ Weight:_____ Pulse:_____
Cross-training:_____
_____
Comments:_____
_____

Friday/Hour: _____ Week of: _____ Week #: _____

Route: _____ Temp./conditions: _____

Ride time: _____ Total time: _____

Distance: _____ Avg. speed: _____ Max. speed: _____

Fitness: _____ Weight: _____ Pulse: _____

Cross-training: _____

Comments: _____

Saturday/Hour: _____ Week of: _____ Week #: _____

Route: _____ Temp./conditions: _____

Ride time: _____ Total time: _____

Distance: _____ Avg. speed: _____ Max. speed: _____

Fitness: _____ Weight: _____ Pulse: _____

Cross-training: _____

Comments: _____

Sunday/Hour: _____ Week of: _____ Week #: _____

Route: _____ Temp./conditions: _____

Ride time: _____ Total time: _____

Distance: _____ Avg. speed: _____ Max. speed: _____

Fitness: _____ Weight: _____ Pulse: _____

Cross-training: _____

Comments: _____

Weekly Summary

Week of: _____ Week #: _____

Goal hours: _____ Total hours: _____ Goal miles: _____ Total miles: _____

Intensity goal: _____ Avg. speed: _____ Max. speed: _____

Fitness: _____ Weight: _____ Pulse: _____

Other training goals: _____

Cross-training: _____

Equipment/Maintenance: _____

Comments: _____

Circuit racer Tom Stevens; Portland, Maine.

Monday/Hour:_____ Week of:_____ Week #:_____

Route:_____ Temp./conditions:_____

Ride time:_____ Total time:_____

Distance:_____ Avg. speed:_____ Max. speed:_____

Fitness:_____ Weight:_____ Pulse:_____

Cross-training:_____

_____

Comments:_____

_____

Tuesday/Hour:_____ Week of:_____ Week #:_____

Route:_____ Temp./conditions:_____

Ride time:_____ Total time:_____

Distance:_____ Avg. speed:_____ Max. speed:_____

Fitness:_____ Weight:_____ Pulse:_____

Cross-training:_____

_____

Comments:_____

_____

Wednesday/Hour:_____ Week of:_____ Week #:_____

Route:_____ Temp./conditions:_____

Ride time:_____ Total time:_____

Distance:_____ Avg. speed:_____ Max. speed:_____

Fitness:_____ Weight:_____ Pulse:_____

Cross-training:_____

_____

Comments:_____

_____

Thursday/Hour:_____ Week of:_____ Week #:_____

Route:_____ Temp./conditions:_____

Ride time:_____ Total time:_____

Distance:_____ Avg. speed:_____ Max. speed:_____

Fitness:_____ Weight:_____ Pulse:_____

Cross-training:_____

_____

Comments:_____

_____

Friday/Hour:_____ Week of:_____ Week #:_____

Route:_____ Temp./conditions:_____

Ride time:_____ Total time:_____

Distance:_____ Avg. speed:_____ Max. speed:_____

Fitness:_____ Weight:_____ Pulse:_____

Cross-training:_____
_____

Comments:_____
_____

Saturday/Hour:_____ Week of:_____ Week #:_____

Route:_____ Temp./conditions:_____

Ride time:_____ Total time:_____

Distance:_____ Avg. speed:_____ Max. speed:_____

Fitness:_____ Weight:_____ Pulse:_____

Cross-training:_____
_____

Comments:_____
_____

Sunday/Hour:_____ Week of:_____ Week #:_____

Route:_____ Temp./conditions:_____

Ride time:_____ Total time:_____

Distance:_____ Avg. speed:_____ Max. speed:_____

Fitness:_____ Weight:_____ Pulse:_____

Cross-training:_____
_____

Comments:_____
_____

Weekly Summary

Week of:_____ Week #:_____

Goal hours:_____ Total hours:_____ Goal miles:_____ Total miles:_____

Intensity goal:_____ Avg. speed:_____ Max. speed:_____

Fitness:_____ Weight:_____ Pulse:_____

Other training goals:_____

Cross-training:_____

Equipment/Maintenance:_____

Comments:_____
_____

43

Monday/Hour:_____ Week of:_____ Week #:_____

Route:_____ Temp./conditions:_____

Ride time:_____ Total time:_____

Distance:_____ Avg. speed:_____ Max. speed:_____

Fitness:_____ Weight:_____ Pulse:_____

Cross-training:_____

Comments:_____

Tuesday/Hour:_____ Week of:_____ Week #:_____

Route:_____ Temp./conditions:_____

Ride time:_____ Total time:_____

Distance:_____ Avg. speed:_____ Max. speed:_____

Fitness:_____ Weight:_____ Pulse:_____

Cross-training:_____

Comments:_____

Wednesday/Hour:_____ Week of:_____ Week #:_____

Route:_____ Temp./conditions:_____

Ride time:_____ Total time:_____

Distance:_____ Avg. speed:_____ Max. speed:_____

Fitness:_____ Weight:_____ Pulse:_____

Cross-training:_____

Comments:_____

Thursday/Hour:_____ Week of:_____ Week #:_____

Route:_____ Temp./conditions:_____

Ride time:_____ Total time:_____

Distance:_____ Avg. speed:_____ Max. speed:_____

Fitness:_____ Weight:_____ Pulse:_____

Cross-training:_____

Comments:_____

Friday/Hour:_____ Week of:_____ Week #:_____

Route:_____ Temp./conditions:_____

Ride time:_____ Total time:_____

Distance:_____ Avg. speed:_____ Max. speed:_____

Fitness:_____ Weight:_____ Pulse:_____

Cross-training:_____

_____

Comments:_____

_____

Saturday/Hour:_____ Week of:_____ Week #:_____

Route:_____ Temp./conditions:_____

Ride time:_____ Total time:_____

Distance:_____ Avg. speed:_____ Max. speed:_____

Fitness:_____ Weight:_____ Pulse:_____

Cross-training:_____

_____

Comments:_____

_____

Sunday/Hour:_____ Week of:_____ Week #:_____

Route:_____ Temp./conditions:_____

Ride time:_____ Total time:_____

Distance:_____ Avg. speed:_____ Max. speed:_____

Fitness:_____ Weight:_____ Pulse:_____

Cross-training:_____

_____

Comments:_____

_____

Weekly Summary

Week of:_____ Week #:_____

Goal hours:_____ Total hours:_____ Goal miles:_____ Total miles:_____

Intensity goal:_____ Avg. speed:_____ Max. speed:_____

Fitness:_____ Weight:_____ Pulse:_____

Other training goals:_____

Cross-training:_____

Equipment/Maintenance:_____

Comments:_____

_____

Monday/Hour:_____ Week of:_____ Week #:_____

Route:_____ Temp./conditions:_____

Ride time:_____ Total time:_____

Distance:_____ Avg. speed:_____ Max. speed:_____

Fitness:_____ Weight:_____ Pulse:_____

Cross-training:_____
_____

Comments:_____
_____

Tuesday/Hour:_____ Week of:_____ Week #:_____

Route:_____ Temp./conditions:_____

Ride time:_____ Total time:_____

Distance:_____ Avg. speed:_____ Max. speed:_____

Fitness:_____ Weight:_____ Pulse:_____

Cross-training:_____
_____

Comments:_____
_____

Wednesday/Hour:_____ Week of:_____ Week #:_____

Route:_____ Temp./conditions:_____

Ride time:_____ Total time:_____

Distance:_____ Avg. speed:_____ Max. speed:_____

Fitness:_____ Weight:_____ Pulse:_____

Cross-training:_____
_____

Comments:_____
_____

Thursday/Hour:_____ Week of:_____ Week #:_____

Route:_____ Temp./conditions:_____

Ride time:_____ Total time:_____

Distance:_____ Avg. speed:_____ Max. speed:_____

Fitness:_____ Weight:_____ Pulse:_____

Cross-training:_____
_____

Comments:_____
_____

Friday/Hour:_____ Week of:_____ Week #:_____

Route:_____ Temp./conditions:_____

Ride time:_____ Total time:_____

Distance:_____ Avg. speed:_____ Max. speed:_____

Fitness:_____ Weight:_____ Pulse:_____

Cross-training:_____

_____

Comments:_____

_____

Saturday/Hour:_____ Week of:_____ Week #:_____

Route:_____ Temp./conditions:_____

Ride time:_____ Total time:_____

Distance:_____ Avg. speed:_____ Max. speed:_____

Fitness:_____ Weight:_____ Pulse:_____

Cross-training:_____

_____

Comments:_____

_____

Sunday/Hour:_____ Week of:_____ Week #:_____

Route:_____ Temp./conditions:_____

Ride time:_____ Total time:_____

Distance:_____ Avg. speed:_____ Max. speed:_____

Fitness:_____ Weight:_____ Pulse:_____

Cross-training:_____

_____

Comments:_____

_____

Weekly Summary

Week of:_____ Week #:_____

Goal hours:_____ Total hours:_____ Goal miles:_____ Total miles:_____

Intensity goal:_____ Avg. speed:_____ Max. speed:_____

Fitness:_____ Weight:_____ Pulse:_____

Other training goals:_____

Cross-training:_____

Equipment/Maintenance:_____

Comments:_____

_____

Monday/Hour:_____ Week of: _____ Week #:_____

Route:_____ Temp./conditions:_____

Ride time: _____ Total time: _____

Distance:_____ Avg. speed: _____ Max. speed:_____

Fitness:_____ Weight: _____ Pulse:_____

Cross-training:_____

_____

Comments:_____

_____

Tuesday/Hour:_____ Week of: _____ Week #:_____

Route:_____ Temp./conditions:_____

Ride time: _____ Total time: _____

Distance:_____ Avg. speed: _____ Max. speed:_____

Fitness:_____ Weight: _____ Pulse:_____

Cross-training:_____

_____

Comments:_____

_____

Wednesday/Hour:_____ Week of: _____ Week #:_____

Route:_____ Temp./conditions:_____

Ride time: _____ Total time: _____

Distance:_____ Avg. speed: _____ Max. speed:_____

Fitness:_____ Weight: _____ Pulse:_____

Cross-training:_____

_____

Comments:_____

_____

Thursday/Hour:_____ Week of: _____ Week #:_____

Route:_____ Temp./conditions:_____

Ride time: _____ Total time: _____

Distance:_____ Avg. speed: _____ Max. speed:_____

Fitness:_____ Weight: _____ Pulse:_____

Cross-training:_____

_____

Comments:_____

_____

Friday/Hour:_____ Week of:_____ Week #:_____

Route:_____ Temp./conditions:_____

Ride time:_____ Total time:_____

Distance:_____ Avg. speed:_____ Max. speed:_____

Fitness:_____ Weight:_____ Pulse:_____

Cross-training:_____

_____

Comments:_____

_____

Saturday/Hour:_____ Week of:_____ Week #:_____

Route:_____ Temp./conditions:_____

Ride time:_____ Total time:_____

Distance:_____ Avg. speed:_____ Max. speed:_____

Fitness:_____ Weight:_____ Pulse:_____

Cross-training:_____

_____

Comments:_____

_____

Sunday/Hour:_____ Week of:_____ Week #:_____

Route:_____ Temp./conditions:_____

Ride time:_____ Total time:_____

Distance:_____ Avg. speed:_____ Max. speed:_____

Fitness:_____ Weight:_____ Pulse:_____

Cross-training:_____

_____

Comments:_____

_____

Weekly Summary

Week of:_____ Week #:_____

Goal hours:_____ Total hours:_____ Goal miles:_____ Total miles:_____

Intensity goal:_____ Avg. speed:_____ Max. speed:_____

Fitness:_____ Weight:_____ Pulse:_____

Other training goals:_____

Cross-training:_____

Equipment/Maintenance:_____

Comments:_____

_____

49

MRC Sterling Road Race; Sterling, Massachusetts.

TRAINING

Monday/Hour:_____ Week of:_____ Week #:_____

Route:_____ Temp./conditions:_____

Ride time:_____ Total time:_____

Distance:_____ Avg. speed:_____ Max. speed:_____

Fitness:_____ Weight:_____ Pulse:_____

Cross-training:_____

Comments:_____

Tuesday/Hour:_____ Week of:_____ Week #:_____

Route:_____ Temp./conditions:_____

Ride time:_____ Total time:_____

Distance:_____ Avg. speed:_____ Max. speed:_____

Fitness:_____ Weight:_____ Pulse:_____

Cross-training:_____

Comments:_____

Wednesday/Hour:_____ Week of:_____ Week #:_____

Route:_____ Temp./conditions:_____

Ride time:_____ Total time:_____

Distance:_____ Avg. speed:_____ Max. speed:_____

Fitness:_____ Weight:_____ Pulse:_____

Cross-training:_____

Comments:_____

Thursday/Hour:_____ Week of:_____ Week #:_____

Route:_____ Temp./conditions:_____

Ride time:_____ Total time:_____

Distance:_____ Avg. speed:_____ Max. speed:_____

Fitness:_____ Weight:_____ Pulse:_____

Cross-training:_____

Comments:_____

Friday/Hour:_____ Week of: _____ Week #:_____

Route:_____ Temp./conditions:_____

Ride time:_____ Total time: _____

Distance:_____ Avg. speed: _____ Max. speed: _____

Fitness:_____ Weight: _____ Pulse:_____

Cross-training:_____

_____

Comments:_____

_____

Saturday/Hour:_____ Week of: _____ Week #:_____

Route:_____ Temp./conditions:_____

Ride time:_____ Total time: _____

Distance:_____ Avg. speed: _____ Max. speed: _____

Fitness:_____ Weight: _____ Pulse:_____

Cross-training:_____

_____

Comments:_____

_____

Sunday/Hour:_____ Week of: _____ Week #:_____

Route:_____ Temp./conditions:_____

Ride time:_____ Total time: _____

Distance:_____ Avg. speed: _____ Max. speed: _____

Fitness:_____ Weight: _____ Pulse:_____

Cross-training:_____

_____

Comments:_____

_____

Weekly Summary

Week of:_____ Week #:_____

Goal hours:_____ Total hours:_____ Goal miles: _____ Total miles:_____

Intensity goal: _____ Avg. speed: _____ Max. speed: _____

Fitness:_____ Weight: _____ Pulse:_____

Other training goals:_____

Cross-training: _____

Equipment/Maintenance:_____

Comments:_____

_____

Monday/Hour:_____ Week of:_____ Week #:_____

Route:_____ Temp./conditions:_____

Ride time:_____ Total time:_____

Distance:_____ Avg. speed:_____ Max. speed:_____

Fitness:_____ Weight:_____ Pulse:_____

Cross-training:_____

Comments:_____

Tuesday/Hour:_____ Week of:_____ Week #:_____

Route:_____ Temp./conditions:_____

Ride time:_____ Total time:_____

Distance:_____ Avg. speed:_____ Max. speed:_____

Fitness:_____ Weight:_____ Pulse:_____

Cross-training:_____

Comments:_____

Wednesday/Hour:_____ Week of:_____ Week #:_____

Route:_____ Temp./conditions:_____

Ride time:_____ Total time:_____

Distance:_____ Avg. speed:_____ Max. speed:_____

Fitness:_____ Weight:_____ Pulse:_____

Cross-training:_____

Comments:_____

Thursday/Hour:_____ Week of:_____ Week #:_____

Route:_____ Temp./conditions:_____

Ride time:_____ Total time:_____

Distance:_____ Avg. speed:_____ Max. speed:_____

Fitness:_____ Weight:_____ Pulse:_____

Cross-training:_____

Comments:_____

TRAINING

Friday/Hour:_____ Week of:_____ Week #:_____

Route:_____ Temp./conditions:_____

Ride time:_____ Total time:_____

Distance:_____ Avg. speed:_____ Max. speed:_____

Fitness:_____ Weight:_____ Pulse:_____

Cross-training:_____

Comments:_____

Saturday/Hour:_____ Week of:_____ Week #:_____

Route:_____ Temp./conditions:_____

Ride time:_____ Total time:_____

Distance:_____ Avg. speed:_____ Max. speed:_____

Fitness:_____ Weight:_____ Pulse:_____

Cross-training:_____

Comments:_____

Sunday/Hour:_____ Week of:_____ Week #:_____

Route:_____ Temp./conditions:_____

Ride time:_____ Total time:_____

Distance:_____ Avg. speed:_____ Max. speed:_____

Fitness:_____ Weight:_____ Pulse:_____

Cross-training:_____

Comments:_____

Weekly Summary

Week of:_____ Week #:_____

Goal hours:_____ Total hours:_____ Goal miles:_____ Total miles:_____

Intensity goal:_____ Avg. speed:_____ Max. speed:_____

Fitness:_____ Weight:_____ Pulse:_____

Other training goals:_____

Cross-training:_____

Equipment/Maintenance:_____

Comments:_____

54

Monday/Hour:_____ Week of:_____ Week #:_____

Route:_____ Temp./conditions:_____

Ride time:_____ Total time:_____

Distance:_____ Avg. speed:_____ Max. speed:_____

Fitness:_____ Weight:_____ Pulse:_____

Cross-training:_____

Comments:_____

_____

Tuesday/Hour:_____ Week of:_____ Week #:_____

Route:_____ Temp./conditions:_____

Ride time:_____ Total time:_____

Distance:_____ Avg. speed:_____ Max. speed:_____

Fitness:_____ Weight:_____ Pulse:_____

Cross-training:_____

Comments:_____

_____

Wednesday/Hour:_____ Week of:_____ Week #:_____

Route:_____ Temp./conditions:_____

Ride time:_____ Total time:_____

Distance:_____ Avg. speed:_____ Max. speed:_____

Fitness:_____ Weight:_____ Pulse:_____

Cross-training:_____

Comments:_____

_____

Thursday/Hour:_____ Week of:_____ Week #:_____

Route:_____ Temp./conditions:_____

Ride time:_____ Total time:_____

Distance:_____ Avg. speed:_____ Max. speed:_____

Fitness:_____ Weight:_____ Pulse:_____

Cross-training:_____

Comments:_____

_____

55

Friday/Hour:_____ Week of:_____ Week #:_____

Route:_____ Temp./conditions:_____

Ride time:_____ Total time:_____

Distance:_____ Avg. speed:_____ Max. speed:_____

Fitness:_____ Weight:_____ Pulse:_____

Cross-training:_____

Comments:_____

_____

Saturday/Hour:_____ Week of:_____ Week #:_____

Route:_____ Temp./conditions:_____

Ride time:_____ Total time:_____

Distance:_____ Avg. speed:_____ Max. speed:_____

Fitness:_____ Weight:_____ Pulse:_____

Cross-training:_____

Comments:_____

_____

Sunday/Hour:_____ Week of:_____ Week #:_____

Route:_____ Temp./conditions:_____

Ride time:_____ Total time:_____

Distance:_____ Avg. speed:_____ Max. speed:_____

Fitness:_____ Weight:_____ Pulse:_____

Cross-training:_____

Comments:_____

_____

Weekly Summary

Week of:_____ Week #:_____

Goal hours:_____ Total hours:_____ Goal miles:_____ Total miles:_____

Intensity goal:_____ Avg. speed:_____ Max. speed:_____

Fitness:_____ Weight:_____ Pulse:_____

Other training goals:_____

Cross-training:_____

Equipment/Maintenance:_____

Comments:_____

_____

Monday/Hour:_____ Week of: _____ Week #:_____

Route:_____ Temp./conditions:_____

Ride time:_____ Total time: _____

Distance:_____ Avg. speed: _____ Max. speed:_____

Fitness:_____ Weight: _____ Pulse:_____

Cross-training:_____

_____

Comments:_____

_____

Tuesday/Hour:_____ Week of: _____ Week #:_____

Route:_____ Temp./conditions:_____

Ride time:_____ Total time: _____

Distance:_____ Avg. speed: _____ Max. speed:_____

Fitness:_____ Weight: _____ Pulse:_____

Cross-training:_____

_____

Comments:_____

_____

Wednesday/Hour:_____ Week of: _____ Week #:_____

Route:_____ Temp./conditions:_____

Ride time:_____ Total time: _____

Distance:_____ Avg. speed: _____ Max. speed:_____

Fitness:_____ Weight: _____ Pulse:_____

Cross-training:_____

_____

Comments:_____

_____

Thursday/Hour:_____ Week of: _____ Week #:_____

Route:_____ Temp./conditions:_____

Ride time:_____ Total time: _____

Distance:_____ Avg. speed: _____ Max. speed:_____

Fitness:_____ Weight: _____ Pulse:_____

Cross-training:_____

_____

Comments:_____

_____

Friday/Hour:_____ Week of:_____ Week #:_____

Route:_____ Temp./conditions:_____

Ride time:_____ Total time:_____

Distance:_____ Avg. speed:_____ Max. speed:_____

Fitness:_____ Weight:_____ Pulse:_____

Cross-training:_____

_____

Comments:_____

_____

Saturday/Hour:_____ Week of:_____ Week #:_____

Route:_____ Temp./conditions:_____

Ride time:_____ Total time:_____

Distance:_____ Avg. speed:_____ Max. speed:_____

Fitness:_____ Weight:_____ Pulse:_____

Cross-training:_____

_____

Comments:_____

_____

Sunday/Hour:_____ Week of:_____ Week #:_____

Route:_____ Temp./conditions:_____

Ride time:_____ Total time:_____

Distance:_____ Avg. speed:_____ Max. speed:_____

Fitness:_____ Weight:_____ Pulse:_____

Cross-training:_____

_____

Comments:_____

_____

Weekly Summary

Week of:_____ Week #:_____

Goal hours:_____ Total hours:_____ Goal miles:_____ Total miles:_____

Intensity goal:_____ Avg. speed:_____ Max. speed:_____

Fitness:_____ Weight:_____ Pulse:_____

Other training goals:_____

Cross-training:_____

Equipment/Maintenance:_____

Comments:_____

_____

Belgian cyclist, practicing at the Sheepshead Bay open air track in preparation for the Six-Day Cycle Race at Madison Square Garden; Brooklyn, New York; 1919.

Monday/Hour:_____ Week of:_____ Week #:_____

Route:_____ Temp./conditions:_____

Ride time:_____ Total time:_____

Distance:_____ Avg. speed:_____ Max. speed:_____

Fitness:_____ Weight:_____ Pulse:_____

Cross-training:_____

Comments:_____

Tuesday/Hour:_____ Week of:_____ Week #:_____

Route:_____ Temp./conditions:_____

Ride time:_____ Total time:_____

Distance:_____ Avg. speed:_____ Max. speed:_____

Fitness:_____ Weight:_____ Pulse:_____

Cross-training:_____

Comments:_____

Wednesday/Hour:_____ Week of:_____ Week #:_____

Route:_____ Temp./conditions:_____

Ride time:_____ Total time:_____

Distance:_____ Avg. speed:_____ Max. speed:_____

Fitness:_____ Weight:_____ Pulse:_____

Cross-training:_____

Comments:_____

Thursday/Hour:_____ Week of:_____ Week #:_____

Route:_____ Temp./conditions:_____

Ride time:_____ Total time:_____

Distance:_____ Avg. speed:_____ Max. speed:_____

Fitness:_____ Weight:_____ Pulse:_____

Cross-training:_____

Comments:_____

Friday/Hour: _____ Week of: _____ Week #: _____

Route: _____ Temp./conditions: _____

Ride time: _____ Total time: _____

Distance: _____ Avg. speed: _____ Max. speed: _____

Fitness: _____ Weight: _____ Pulse: _____

Cross-training: _____

_____

Comments: _____

_____

Saturday/Hour: _____ Week of: _____ Week #: _____

Route: _____ Temp./conditions: _____

Ride time: _____ Total time: _____

Distance: _____ Avg. speed: _____ Max. speed: _____

Fitness: _____ Weight: _____ Pulse: _____

Cross-training: _____

_____

Comments: _____

_____

Sunday/Hour: _____ Week of: _____ Week #: _____

Route: _____ Temp./conditions: _____

Ride time: _____ Total time: _____

Distance: _____ Avg. speed: _____ Max. speed: _____

Fitness: _____ Weight: _____ Pulse: _____

Cross-training: _____

_____

Comments: _____

_____

Weekly Summary

Week of: _____ Week #: _____

Goal hours: _____ Total hours: _____ Goal miles: _____ Total miles: _____

Intensity goal: _____ Avg. speed: _____ Max. speed: _____

Fitness: _____ Weight: _____ Pulse: _____

Other training goals: _____

Cross-training: _____

Equipment/Maintenance: _____

Comments: _____

_____

61

TRAINING

Monday/Hour:_____ Week of:_____ Week #:_____

Route:_____ Temp./conditions:_____

Ride time:_____ Total time:_____

Distance:_____ Avg. speed:_____ Max. speed:_____

Fitness:_____ Weight:_____ Pulse:_____

Cross-training:_____

Comments:_____

Tuesday/Hour:_____ Week of:_____ Week #:_____

Route:_____ Temp./conditions:_____

Ride time:_____ Total time:_____

Distance:_____ Avg. speed:_____ Max. speed:_____

Fitness:_____ Weight:_____ Pulse:_____

Cross-training:_____

Comments:_____

Wednesday/Hour:_____ Week of:_____ Week #:_____

Route:_____ Temp./conditions:_____

Ride time:_____ Total time:_____

Distance:_____ Avg. speed:_____ Max. speed:_____

Fitness:_____ Weight:_____ Pulse:_____

Cross-training:_____

Comments:_____

Thursday/Hour:_____ Week of:_____ Week #:_____

Route:_____ Temp./conditions:_____

Ride time:_____ Total time:_____

Distance:_____ Avg. speed:_____ Max. speed:_____

Fitness:_____ Weight:_____ Pulse:_____

Cross-training:_____

Comments:_____

Friday/Hour:_____ Week of:_____ Week #:_____

Route:_____ Temp./conditions:_____

Ride time:_____ Total time:_____

Distance:_____ Avg. speed:_____ Max. speed:_____

Fitness:_____ Weight:_____ Pulse:_____

Cross-training:_____

Comments:_____
_____

Saturday/Hour:_____ Week of:_____ Week #:_____

Route:_____ Temp./conditions:_____

Ride time:_____ Total time:_____

Distance:_____ Avg. speed:_____ Max. speed:_____

Fitness:_____ Weight:_____ Pulse:_____

Cross-training:_____

Comments:_____
_____

Sunday/Hour:_____ Week of:_____ Week #:_____

Route:_____ Temp./conditions:_____

Ride time:_____ Total time:_____

Distance:_____ Avg. speed:_____ Max. speed:_____

Fitness:_____ Weight:_____ Pulse:_____

Cross-training:_____

Comments:_____
_____

Weekly Summary

Week of:_____ Week #:_____

Goal hours:_____ Total hours:_____ Goal miles:_____ Total miles:_____

Intensity goal:_____ Avg. speed:_____ Max. speed:_____

Fitness:_____ Weight:_____ Pulse:_____

Other training goals:_____

Cross-training:_____

Equipment/Maintenance:_____

Comments:_____
_____

63

Monday/Hour:_____ Week of: _____ Week #:_____

Route:_____ Temp./conditions:_____

Ride time: _____ Total time: _____

Distance:_____ Avg. speed: _____ Max. speed:_____

Fitness:_____ Weight: _____ Pulse:_____

Cross-training:_____

Comments:_____

Tuesday/Hour:_____ Week of: _____ Week #:_____

Route:_____ Temp./conditions:_____

Ride time: _____ Total time: _____

Distance:_____ Avg. speed: _____ Max. speed:_____

Fitness:_____ Weight: _____ Pulse:_____

Cross-training:_____

Comments:_____

Wednesday/Hour:_____ Week of: _____ Week #:_____

Route:_____ Temp./conditions:_____

Ride time: _____ Total time: _____

Distance:_____ Avg. speed: _____ Max. speed:_____

Fitness:_____ Weight: _____ Pulse:_____

Cross-training:_____

Comments:_____

Thursday/Hour:_____ Week of: _____ Week #:_____

Route:_____ Temp./conditions:_____

Ride time: _____ Total time: _____

Distance:_____ Avg. speed: _____ Max. speed:_____

Fitness:_____ Weight: _____ Pulse:_____

Cross-training:_____

Comments:_____

Friday/Hour:_____ Week of:_____ Week #:_____

Route:_____ Temp./conditions:_____

Ride time:_____ Total time:_____

Distance:_____ Avg. speed:_____ Max. speed:_____

Fitness:_____ Weight:_____ Pulse:_____

Cross-training:_____

_____

Comments:_____

_____

Saturday/Hour:_____ Week of:_____ Week #:_____

Route:_____ Temp./conditions:_____

Ride time:_____ Total time:_____

Distance:_____ Avg. speed:_____ Max. speed:_____

Fitness:_____ Weight:_____ Pulse:_____

Cross-training:_____

_____

Comments:_____

_____

Sunday/Hour:_____ Week of:_____ Week #:_____

Route:_____ Temp./conditions:_____

Ride time:_____ Total time:_____

Distance:_____ Avg. speed:_____ Max. speed:_____

Fitness:_____ Weight:_____ Pulse:_____

Cross-training:_____

_____

Comments:_____

_____

Weekly Summary

Week of:_____ Week #:_____

Goal hours:_____ Total hours:_____ Goal miles:_____ Total miles:_____

Intensity goal:_____ Avg. speed:_____ Max. speed:_____

Fitness:_____ Weight:_____ Pulse:_____

Other training goals:_____

Cross-training:_____

Equipment/Maintenance:_____

Comments:_____

_____

65

Monday/Hour:_____ Week of:_____ Week #:_____

Route:_____ Temp./conditions:_____

Ride time:_____ Total time:_____

Distance:_____ Avg. speed:_____ Max. speed:_____

Fitness:_____ Weight:_____ Pulse:_____

Cross-training:_____

Comments:_____

Tuesday/Hour:_____ Week of:_____ Week #:_____

Route:_____ Temp./conditions:_____

Ride time:_____ Total time:_____

Distance:_____ Avg. speed:_____ Max. speed:_____

Fitness:_____ Weight:_____ Pulse:_____

Cross-training:_____

Comments:_____

Wednesday/Hour:_____ Week of:_____ Week #:_____

Route:_____ Temp./conditions:_____

Ride time:_____ Total time:_____

Distance:_____ Avg. speed:_____ Max. speed:_____

Fitness:_____ Weight:_____ Pulse:_____

Cross-training:_____

Comments:_____

Thursday/Hour:_____ Week of:_____ Week #:_____

Route:_____ Temp./conditions:_____

Ride time:_____ Total time:_____

Distance:_____ Avg. speed:_____ Max. speed:_____

Fitness:_____ Weight:_____ Pulse:_____

Cross-training:_____

Comments:_____

Friday/Hour:_____ Week of:_____ Week #:_____

Route:_____ Temp./conditions:_____

Ride time:_____ Total time:_____

Distance:_____ Avg. speed:_____ Max. speed:_____

Fitness:_____ Weight:_____ Pulse:_____

Cross-training:_____

Comments:_____
_____

Saturday/Hour:_____ Week of:_____ Week #:_____

Route:_____ Temp./conditions:_____

Ride time:_____ Total time:_____

Distance:_____ Avg. speed:_____ Max. speed:_____

Fitness:_____ Weight:_____ Pulse:_____

Cross-training:_____

Comments:_____
_____

Sunday/Hour:_____ Week of:_____ Week #:_____

Route:_____ Temp./conditions:_____

Ride time:_____ Total time:_____

Distance:_____ Avg. speed:_____ Max. speed:_____

Fitness:_____ Weight:_____ Pulse:_____

Cross-training:_____

Comments:_____
_____

Weekly Summary

Week of:_____ Week #:_____

Goal hours:_____ Total hours:_____ Goal miles:_____ Total miles:_____

Intensity goal:_____ Avg. speed:_____ Max. speed:_____

Fitness:_____ Weight:_____ Pulse:_____

Other training goals:_____

Cross-training:_____

Equipment/Maintenance:_____

Comments:_____
_____

Start of the semi-annual Six-Day Cycle Race at Madison Square Garden; New York; 1927.

Monday/Hour:_____ Week of: _____ Week #:_____

Route:_____ Temp./conditions:_____

Ride time: _____ Total time: _____

Distance:_____ Avg. speed: _____ Max. speed:_____

Fitness:_____ Weight: _____ Pulse:_____

Cross-training:_____

Comments:_____

Tuesday/Hour:_____ Week of: _____ Week #:_____

Route:_____ Temp./conditions:_____

Ride time: _____ Total time: _____

Distance:_____ Avg. speed: _____ Max. speed:_____

Fitness:_____ Weight: _____ Pulse:_____

Cross-training:_____

Comments:_____

Wednesday/Hour:_____ Week of: _____ Week #:_____

Route:_____ Temp./conditions:_____

Ride time: _____ Total time: _____

Distance:_____ Avg. speed: _____ Max. speed:_____

Fitness:_____ Weight: _____ Pulse:_____

Cross-training:_____

Comments:_____

Thursday/Hour:_____ Week of: _____ Week #:_____

Route:_____ Temp./conditions:_____

Ride time: _____ Total time: _____

Distance:_____ Avg. speed: _____ Max. speed:_____

Fitness:_____ Weight: _____ Pulse:_____

Cross-training:_____

Comments:_____

TRAINING

Friday/Hour: _____ Week of: _____ Week #: _____

Route: _____ Temp./conditions: _____

Ride time: _____ Total time: _____

Distance: _____ Avg. speed: _____ Max. speed: _____

Fitness: _____ Weight: _____ Pulse: _____

Cross-training: _____

Comments: _____

Saturday/Hour: _____ Week of: _____ Week #: _____

Route: _____ Temp./conditions: _____

Ride time: _____ Total time: _____

Distance: _____ Avg. speed: _____ Max. speed: _____

Fitness: _____ Weight: _____ Pulse: _____

Cross-training: _____

Comments: _____

Sunday/Hour: _____ Week of: _____ Week #: _____

Route: _____ Temp./conditions: _____

Ride time: _____ Total time: _____

Distance: _____ Avg. speed: _____ Max. speed: _____

Fitness: _____ Weight: _____ Pulse: _____

Cross-training: _____

Comments: _____

Weekly Summary

Week of: _____ Week #: _____

Goal hours: _____ Total hours: _____ Goal miles: _____ Total miles: _____

Intensity goal: _____ Avg. speed: _____ Max. speed: _____

Fitness: _____ Weight: _____ Pulse: _____

Other training goals: _____

Cross-training: _____

Equipment/Maintenance: _____

Comments: _____

Monday/Hour:_____ Week of: _____ Week #:_____

Route:_____ Temp./conditions:_____

Ride time:_____ Total time: _____

Distance:_____ Avg. speed: _____ Max. speed:_____

Fitness:_____ Weight: _____ Pulse:_____

Cross-training:_____

Comments:_____

Tuesday/Hour:_____ Week of: _____ Week #:_____

Route:_____ Temp./conditions:_____

Ride time:_____ Total time: _____

Distance:_____ Avg. speed: _____ Max. speed:_____

Fitness:_____ Weight: _____ Pulse:_____

Cross-training:_____

Comments:_____

Wednesday/Hour:_____ Week of: _____ Week #:_____

Route:_____ Temp./conditions:_____

Ride time:_____ Total time: _____

Distance:_____ Avg. speed: _____ Max. speed:_____

Fitness:_____ Weight: _____ Pulse:_____

Cross-training:_____

Comments:_____

Thursday/Hour:_____ Week of: _____ Week #:_____

Route:_____ Temp./conditions:_____

Ride time:_____ Total time: _____

Distance:_____ Avg. speed: _____ Max. speed:_____

Fitness:_____ Weight: _____ Pulse:_____

Cross-training:_____

Comments:_____

Friday/Hour:_____ Week of:_____ Week #:_____

Route:_____ Temp./conditions:_____

Ride time:_____ Total time:_____

Distance:_____ Avg. speed:_____ Max. speed:_____

Fitness:_____ Weight:_____ Pulse:_____

Cross-training:_____

_____

Comments:_____

_____

Saturday/Hour:_____ Week of:_____ Week #:_____

Route:_____ Temp./conditions:_____

Ride time:_____ Total time:_____

Distance:_____ Avg. speed:_____ Max. speed:_____

Fitness:_____ Weight:_____ Pulse:_____

Cross-training:_____

_____

Comments:_____

_____

Sunday/Hour:_____ Week of:_____ Week #:_____

Route:_____ Temp./conditions:_____

Ride time:_____ Total time:_____

Distance:_____ Avg. speed:_____ Max. speed:_____

Fitness:_____ Weight:_____ Pulse:_____

Cross-training:_____

_____

Comments:_____

_____

Weekly Summary

Week of:_____ Week #:_____

Goal hours:_____ Total hours:_____ Goal miles:_____ Total miles:_____

Intensity goal:_____ Avg. speed:_____ Max. speed:_____

Fitness:_____ Weight:_____ Pulse:_____

Other training goals:_____

Cross-training:_____

Equipment/Maintenance:_____

Comments:_____

_____

Monday/Hour:_____ Week of:_____ Week #:_____

Route:_____ Temp./conditions:_____

Ride time:_____ Total time:_____

Distance:_____ Avg. speed:_____ Max. speed:_____

Fitness:_____ Weight:_____ Pulse:_____

Cross-training:_____

_____

Comments:_____

_____

Tuesday/Hour:_____ Week of:_____ Week #:_____

Route:_____ Temp./conditions:_____

Ride time:_____ Total time:_____

Distance:_____ Avg. speed:_____ Max. speed:_____

Fitness:_____ Weight:_____ Pulse:_____

Cross-training:_____

_____

Comments:_____

_____

Wednesday/Hour:_____ Week of:_____ Week #:_____

Route:_____ Temp./conditions:_____

Ride time:_____ Total time:_____

Distance:_____ Avg. speed:_____ Max. speed:_____

Fitness:_____ Weight:_____ Pulse:_____

Cross-training:_____

_____

Comments:_____

_____

Thursday/Hour:_____ Week of:_____ Week #:_____

Route:_____ Temp./conditions:_____

Ride time:_____ Total time:_____

Distance:_____ Avg. speed:_____ Max. speed:_____

Fitness:_____ Weight:_____ Pulse:_____

Cross-training:_____

_____

Comments:_____

_____

Friday/Hour:_____ Week of:_____ Week #:_____

Route:_____ Temp./conditions:_____

Ride time:_____ Total time:_____

Distance:_____ Avg. speed:_____ Max. speed:_____

Fitness:_____ Weight:_____ Pulse:_____

Cross-training:_____

_____

Comments:_____

_____

Saturday/Hour:_____ Week of:_____ Week #:_____

Route:_____ Temp./conditions:_____

Ride time:_____ Total time:_____

Distance:_____ Avg. speed:_____ Max. speed:_____

Fitness:_____ Weight:_____ Pulse:_____

Cross-training:_____

_____

Comments:_____

_____

Sunday/Hour:_____ Week of:_____ Week #:_____

Route:_____ Temp./conditions:_____

Ride time:_____ Total time:_____

Distance:_____ Avg. speed:_____ Max. speed:_____

Fitness:_____ Weight:_____ Pulse:_____

Cross-training:_____

_____

Comments:_____

_____

Weekly Summary

Week of:_____ Week #:_____

Goal hours:_____ Total hours:_____ Goal miles:_____ Total miles:_____

Intensity goal:_____ Avg. speed:_____ Max. speed:_____

Fitness:_____ Weight:_____ Pulse:_____

Other training goals:_____

Cross-training:_____

Equipment/Maintenance:_____

Comments:_____

_____

Monday/Hour:_____ Week of:_____ Week #:_____
Route:_____ Temp./conditions:_____
Ride time:_____ Total time:_____
Distance:_____ Avg. speed:_____ Max. speed:_____
Fitness:_____ Weight:_____ Pulse:_____
Cross-training:_____

Comments:_____

Tuesday/Hour:_____ Week of:_____ Week #:_____
Route:_____ Temp./conditions:_____
Ride time:_____ Total time:_____
Distance:_____ Avg. speed:_____ Max. speed:_____
Fitness:_____ Weight:_____ Pulse:_____
Cross-training:_____

Comments:_____

Wednesday/Hour:_____ Week of:_____ Week #:_____
Route:_____ Temp./conditions:_____
Ride time:_____ Total time:_____
Distance:_____ Avg. speed:_____ Max. speed:_____
Fitness:_____ Weight:_____ Pulse:_____
Cross-training:_____

Comments:_____

Thursday/Hour:_____ Week of:_____ Week #:_____
Route:_____ Temp./conditions:_____
Ride time:_____ Total time:_____
Distance:_____ Avg. speed:_____ Max. speed:_____
Fitness:_____ Weight:_____ Pulse:_____
Cross-training:_____

Comments:_____

Friday/Hour:_____ Week of: _____ Week #:_____

Route:_____ Temp./conditions:_____

Ride time:_____ Total time: _____

Distance:_____ Avg. speed: _____ Max. speed:_____

Fitness:_____ Weight: _____ Pulse:_____

Cross-training:_____

_____

Comments:_____

_____

Saturday/Hour:_____ Week of: _____ Week #:_____

Route:_____ Temp./conditions:_____

Ride time:_____ Total time: _____

Distance:_____ Avg. speed: _____ Max. speed:_____

Fitness:_____ Weight: _____ Pulse:_____

Cross-training:_____

_____

Comments:_____

_____

Sunday/Hour:_____ Week of: _____ Week #:_____

Route:_____ Temp./conditions:_____

Ride time:_____ Total time: _____

Distance:_____ Avg. speed: _____ Max. speed:_____

Fitness:_____ Weight: _____ Pulse:_____

Cross-training:_____

_____

Comments:_____

_____

Weekly Summary

Week of:_____ Week #:_____

Goal hours:_____ Total hours:_____ Goal miles: _____ Total miles:_____

Intensity goal: _____ Avg. speed: _____ Max. speed: _____

Fitness:_____ Weight: _____ Pulse: _____

Other training goals:_____

Cross-training: _____

Equipment/Maintenance:_____

Comments:_____

_____

Andy Mills during the Rutland Criterium/Killington Stage Race, Junior division; Rutland, Vermont.

Monday/Hour:_____ Week of:_____ Week #:_____

Route:_____ Temp./conditions:_____

Ride time:_____ Total time:_____

Distance:_____ Avg. speed:_____ Max. speed:_____

Fitness:_____ Weight:_____ Pulse:_____

Cross-training:_____

_____

Comments:_____

_____

Tuesday/Hour:_____ Week of:_____ Week #:_____

Route:_____ Temp./conditions:_____

Ride time:_____ Total time:_____

Distance:_____ Avg. speed:_____ Max. speed:_____

Fitness:_____ Weight:_____ Pulse:_____

Cross-training:_____

_____

Comments:_____

_____

Wednesday/Hour:_____ Week of:_____ Week #:_____

Route:_____ Temp./conditions:_____

Ride time:_____ Total time:_____

Distance:_____ Avg. speed:_____ Max. speed:_____

Fitness:_____ Weight:_____ Pulse:_____

Cross-training:_____

_____

Comments:_____

_____

Thursday/Hour:_____ Week of:_____ Week #:_____

Route:_____ Temp./conditions:_____

Ride time:_____ Total time:_____

Distance:_____ Avg. speed:_____ Max. speed:_____

Fitness:_____ Weight:_____ Pulse:_____

Cross-training:_____

_____

Comments:_____

_____

Friday/Hour:_____ Week of:_____ Week #:_____

Route:_____ Temp./conditions:_____

Ride time:_____ Total time:_____

Distance:_____ Avg. speed:_____ Max. speed:_____

Fitness:_____ Weight:_____ Pulse:_____

Cross-training:_____

Comments:_____

Saturday/Hour:_____ Week of:_____ Week #:_____

Route:_____ Temp./conditions:_____

Ride time:_____ Total time:_____

Distance:_____ Avg. speed:_____ Max. speed:_____

Fitness:_____ Weight:_____ Pulse:_____

Cross-training:_____

Comments:_____

Sunday/Hour:_____ Week of:_____ Week #:_____

Route:_____ Temp./conditions:_____

Ride time:_____ Total time:_____

Distance:_____ Avg. speed:_____ Max. speed:_____

Fitness:_____ Weight:_____ Pulse:_____

Cross-training:_____

Comments:_____

Weekly Summary

Week of:_____ Week #:_____

Goal hours:_____ Total hours:_____ Goal miles:_____ Total miles:_____

Intensity goal:_____ Avg. speed:_____ Max. speed:_____

Fitness:_____ Weight:_____ Pulse:_____

Other training goals:_____

Cross-training:_____

Equipment/Maintenance:_____

Comments:_____

Monday/Hour:_____ Week of:_____ Week #:_____

Route:_____ Temp./conditions:_____

Ride time:_____ Total time:_____

Distance:_____ Avg. speed:_____ Max. speed:_____

Fitness:_____ Weight:_____ Pulse:_____

Cross-training:_____

Comments:_____

Tuesday/Hour:_____ Week of:_____ Week #:_____

Route:_____ Temp./conditions:_____

Ride time:_____ Total time:_____

Distance:_____ Avg. speed:_____ Max. speed:_____

Fitness:_____ Weight:_____ Pulse:_____

Cross-training:_____

Comments:_____

Wednesday/Hour:_____ Week of:_____ Week #:_____

Route:_____ Temp./conditions:_____

Ride time:_____ Total time:_____

Distance:_____ Avg. speed:_____ Max. speed:_____

Fitness:_____ Weight:_____ Pulse:_____

Cross-training:_____

Comments:_____

Thursday/Hour:_____ Week of:_____ Week #:_____

Route:_____ Temp./conditions:_____

Ride time:_____ Total time:_____

Distance:_____ Avg. speed:_____ Max. speed:_____

Fitness:_____ Weight:_____ Pulse:_____

Cross-training:_____

Comments:_____

Friday/Hour:_____ Week of: _____ Week #:_____

Route:_____ Temp./conditions:_____

Ride time: _____ Total time: _____

Distance:_____ Avg. speed: _____ Max. speed:_____

Fitness:_____ Weight: _____ Pulse:_____

Cross-training:_____

_____

Comments:_____

_____

Saturday/Hour:_____ Week of: _____ Week #:_____

Route:_____ Temp./conditions:_____

Ride time: _____ Total time: _____

Distance:_____ Avg. speed: _____ Max. speed:_____

Fitness:_____ Weight: _____ Pulse:_____

Cross-training:_____

Comments:_____

_____

Sunday/Hour:_____ Week of: _____ Week #:_____

Route:_____ Temp./conditions:_____

Ride time: _____ Total time: _____

Distance:_____ Avg. speed: _____ Max. speed:_____

Fitness:_____ Weight: _____ Pulse:_____

Cross-training:_____

_____

Comments:_____

_____

Weekly Summary

Week of:_____ Week #:_____

Goal hours:_____ Total hours: _____ Goal miles: _____ Total miles:_____

Intensity goal: _____ Avg. speed: _____ Max. speed: _____

Fitness:_____ Weight: _____ Pulse: _____

Other training goals:_____

Cross-training: _____

Equipment/Maintenance:_____

Comments:_____

_____

Monday/Hour:_____ Week of:_____ Week #:_____

Route:_____ Temp./conditions:_____

Ride time:_____ Total time:_____

Distance:_____ Avg. speed:_____ Max. speed:_____

Fitness:_____ Weight:_____ Pulse:_____

Cross-training:_____

_____

Comments:_____

_____

Tuesday/Hour:_____ Week of:_____ Week #:_____

Route:_____ Temp./conditions:_____

Ride time:_____ Total time:_____

Distance:_____ Avg. speed:_____ Max. speed:_____

Fitness:_____ Weight:_____ Pulse:_____

Cross-training:_____

_____

Comments:_____

_____

Wednesday/Hour:_____ Week of:_____ Week #:_____

Route:_____ Temp./conditions:_____

Ride time:_____ Total time:_____

Distance:_____ Avg. speed:_____ Max. speed:_____

Fitness:_____ Weight:_____ Pulse:_____

Cross-training:_____

_____

Comments:_____

_____

Thursday/Hour:_____ Week of:_____ Week #:_____

Route:_____ Temp./conditions:_____

Ride time:_____ Total time:_____

Distance:_____ Avg. speed:_____ Max. speed:_____

Fitness:_____ Weight:_____ Pulse:_____

Cross-training:_____

_____

Comments:_____

_____

Friday/Hour:_____ Week of:_____ Week #:_____

Route:_____ Temp./conditions:_____

Ride time:_____ Total time:_____

Distance:_____ Avg. speed:_____ Max. speed:_____

Fitness:_____ Weight:_____ Pulse:_____

Cross-training:_____

_____

Comments:_____

_____

Saturday/Hour:_____ Week of:_____ Week #:_____

Route:_____ Temp./conditions:_____

Ride time:_____ Total time:_____

Distance:_____ Avg. speed:_____ Max. speed:_____

Fitness:_____ Weight:_____ Pulse:_____

Cross-training:_____

_____

Comments:_____

_____

Sunday/Hour:_____ Week of:_____ Week #:_____

Route:_____ Temp./conditions:_____

Ride time:_____ Total time:_____

Distance:_____ Avg. speed:_____ Max. speed:_____

Fitness:_____ Weight:_____ Pulse:_____

Cross-training:_____

_____

Comments:_____

_____

Weekly Summary

Week of:_____ Week #:_____

Goal hours:_____ Total hours:_____ Goal miles:_____ Total miles:_____

Intensity goal:_____ Avg. speed:_____ Max. speed:_____

Fitness:_____ Weight:_____ Pulse:_____

Other training goals:_____

Cross-training:_____

Equipment/Maintenance:_____

Comments:_____

_____

83

Monday/Hour:_____ Week of:_____ Week #:_____

Route:_____ Temp./conditions:_____

Ride time:_____ Total time:_____

Distance:_____ Avg. speed:_____ Max. speed:_____

Fitness:_____ Weight:_____ Pulse:_____

Cross-training:_____

Comments:_____

Tuesday/Hour:_____ Week of:_____ Week #:_____

Route:_____ Temp./conditions:_____

Ride time:_____ Total time:_____

Distance:_____ Avg. speed:_____ Max. speed:_____

Fitness:_____ Weight:_____ Pulse:_____

Cross-training:_____

Comments:_____

Wednesday/Hour:_____ Week of:_____ Week #:_____

Route:_____ Temp./conditions:_____

Ride time:_____ Total time:_____

Distance:_____ Avg. speed:_____ Max. speed:_____

Fitness:_____ Weight:_____ Pulse:_____

Cross-training:_____

Comments:_____

Thursday/Hour:_____ Week of:_____ Week #:_____

Route:_____ Temp./conditions:_____

Ride time:_____ Total time:_____

Distance:_____ Avg. speed:_____ Max. speed:_____

Fitness:_____ Weight:_____ Pulse:_____

Cross-training:_____

Comments:_____

Friday/Hour:_____ Week of:_____ Week #:_____

Route:_____ Temp./conditions:_____

Ride time:_____ Total time:_____

Distance:_____ Avg. speed:_____ Max. speed:_____

Fitness:_____ Weight:_____ Pulse:_____

Cross-training:_____

Comments:_____

Saturday/Hour:_____ Week of:_____ Week #:_____

Route:_____ Temp./conditions:_____

Ride time:_____ Total time:_____

Distance:_____ Avg. speed:_____ Max. speed:_____

Fitness:_____ Weight:_____ Pulse:_____

Cross-training:_____

Comments:_____

Sunday/Hour:_____ Week of:_____ Week #:_____

Route:_____ Temp./conditions:_____

Ride time:_____ Total time:_____

Distance:_____ Avg. speed:_____ Max. speed:_____

Fitness:_____ Weight:_____ Pulse:_____

Cross-training:_____

Comments:_____

Weekly Summary

Week of:_____ Week #:_____

Goal hours:_____ Total hours:_____ Goal miles:_____ Total miles:_____

Intensity goal:_____ Avg. speed:_____ Max. speed:_____

Fitness:_____ Weight:_____ Pulse:_____

Other training goals:_____

Cross-training:_____

Equipment/Maintenance:_____

Comments:_____

Rebecca Twigg-Whitehead of the U.S. raises her arms in victory after winning the Individual Road Race event in Pan Am Games bicycle action.

Monday/Hour:_____ Week of:_____ Week #:_____

Route:_____ Temp./conditions:_____

Ride time:_____ Total time:_____

Distance:_____ Avg. speed:_____ Max. speed:_____

Fitness:_____ Weight:_____ Pulse:_____

Cross-training:_____

Comments:_____
_____

Tuesday/Hour:_____ Week of:_____ Week #:_____

Route:_____ Temp./conditions:_____

Ride time:_____ Total time:_____

Distance:_____ Avg. speed:_____ Max. speed:_____

Fitness:_____ Weight:_____ Pulse:_____

Cross-training:_____

Comments:_____
_____

Wednesday/Hour:_____ Week of:_____ Week #:_____

Route:_____ Temp./conditions:_____

Ride time:_____ Total time:_____

Distance:_____ Avg. speed:_____ Max. speed:_____

Fitness:_____ Weight:_____ Pulse:_____

Cross-training:_____

Comments:_____
_____

Thursday/Hour:_____ Week of:_____ Week #:_____

Route:_____ Temp./conditions:_____

Ride time:_____ Total time:_____

Distance:_____ Avg. speed:_____ Max. speed:_____

Fitness:_____ Weight:_____ Pulse:_____

Cross-training:_____

Comments:_____
_____

TRAINING

Friday/Hour:_____ Week of:_____ Week #:_____

Route:_____ Temp./conditions:_____

Ride time:_____ Total time: _____

Distance:_____ Avg. speed: _____ Max. speed:_____

Fitness:_____ Weight: _____ Pulse:_____

Cross-training:_____
_____

Comments:_____
_____

Saturday/Hour:_____ Week of:_____ Week #:_____

Route:_____ Temp./conditions:_____

Ride time:_____ Total time: _____

Distance:_____ Avg. speed: _____ Max. speed:_____

Fitness:_____ Weight: _____ Pulse:_____

Cross-training:_____
_____

Comments:_____
_____

Sunday/Hour:_____ Week of:_____ Week #:_____

Route:_____ Temp./conditions:_____

Ride time:_____ Total time: _____

Distance:_____ Avg. speed: _____ Max. speed:_____

Fitness:_____ Weight: _____ Pulse:_____

Cross-training:_____
_____

Comments:_____
_____

Weekly Summary

Week of:_____ Week #:_____

Goal hours:_____ Total hours:_____ Goal miles: _____ Total miles:_____

Intensity goal: _____ Avg. speed: _____ Max. speed:_____

Fitness:_____ Weight: _____ Pulse:_____

Other training goals:_____

Cross-training: _____

Equipment/Maintenance: _____

Comments:_____
_____

Monday/Hour:_____ Week of:_____ Week #:_____

Route:_____ Temp./conditions:_____

Ride time:_____ Total time:_____

Distance:_____ Avg. speed:_____ Max. speed:_____

Fitness:_____ Weight:_____ Pulse:_____

Cross-training:_____

_____

Comments:_____

_____

Tuesday/Hour:_____ Week of:_____ Week #:_____

Route:_____ Temp./conditions:_____

Ride time:_____ Total time:_____

Distance:_____ Avg. speed:_____ Max. speed:_____

Fitness:_____ Weight:_____ Pulse:_____

Cross-training:_____

_____

Comments:_____

_____

Wednesday/Hour:_____ Week of:_____ Week #:_____

Route:_____ Temp./conditions:_____

Ride time:_____ Total time:_____

Distance:_____ Avg. speed:_____ Max. speed:_____

Fitness:_____ Weight:_____ Pulse:_____

Cross-training:_____

_____

Comments:_____

_____

Thursday/Hour:_____ Week of:_____ Week #:_____

Route:_____ Temp./conditions:_____

Ride time:_____ Total time:_____

Distance:_____ Avg. speed:_____ Max. speed:_____

Fitness:_____ Weight:_____ Pulse:_____

Cross-training:_____

_____

Comments:_____

_____

Friday/Hour:_____ Week of:_____ Week #:_____

Route:_____ Temp./conditions:_____

Ride time:_____ Total time:_____

Distance:_____ Avg. speed:_____ Max. speed:_____

Fitness:_____ Weight:_____ Pulse:_____

Cross-training:_____

_____

Comments:_____

_____

Saturday/Hour:_____ Week of:_____ Week #:_____

Route:_____ Temp./conditions:_____

Ride time:_____ Total time:_____

Distance:_____ Avg. speed:_____ Max. speed:_____

Fitness:_____ Weight:_____ Pulse:_____

Cross-training:_____

_____

Comments:_____

_____

Sunday/Hour:_____ Week of:_____ Week #:_____

Route:_____ Temp./conditions:_____

Ride time:_____ Total time:_____

Distance:_____ Avg. speed:_____ Max. speed:_____

Fitness:_____ Weight:_____ Pulse:_____

Cross-training:_____

_____

Comments:_____

_____

Weekly Summary

Week of:_____ Week #:_____

Goal hours:_____ Total hours:_____ Goal miles:_____ Total miles:_____

Intensity goal:_____ Avg. speed:_____ Max. speed:_____

Fitness:_____ Weight:_____ Pulse:_____

Other training goals:_____

Cross-training:_____

Equipment/Maintenance:_____

Comments:_____

_____

Monday/Hour:_____ Week of: _____ Week #:_____

Route:_____ Temp./conditions:_____

Ride time:_____ Total time: _____

Distance:_____ Avg. speed: _____ Max. speed:_____

Fitness:_____ Weight: _____ Pulse:_____

Cross-training:_____
_____

Comments:_____
_____

Tuesday/Hour:_____ Week of: _____ Week #:_____

Route:_____ Temp./conditions:_____

Ride time:_____ Total time: _____

Distance:_____ Avg. speed: _____ Max. speed:_____

Fitness:_____ Weight: _____ Pulse:_____

Cross-training:_____

Comments:_____
_____

Wednesday/Hour:_____ Week of: _____ Week #:_____

Route:_____ Temp./conditions:_____

Ride time:_____ Total time: _____

Distance:_____ Avg. speed: _____ Max. speed:_____

Fitness:_____ Weight: _____ Pulse:_____

Cross-training:_____

Comments:_____
_____

Thursday/Hour:_____ Week of: _____ Week #:_____

Route:_____ Temp./conditions:_____

Ride time:_____ Total time: _____

Distance:_____ Avg. speed: _____ Max. speed:_____

Fitness:_____ Weight: _____ Pulse:_____

Cross-training:_____

Comments:_____
_____

Friday/Hour: _____ Week of: _____ Week #: _____

Route: _____ Temp./conditions: _____

Ride time: _____ Total time: _____

Distance: _____ Avg. speed: _____ Max. speed: _____

Fitness: _____ Weight: _____ Pulse: _____

Cross-training: _____

_____

Comments: _____

_____

Saturday/Hour: _____ Week of: _____ Week #: _____

Route: _____ Temp./conditions: _____

Ride time: _____ Total time: _____

Distance: _____ Avg. speed: _____ Max. speed: _____

Fitness: _____ Weight: _____ Pulse: _____

Cross-training: _____

_____

Comments: _____

_____

Sunday/Hour: _____ Week of: _____ Week #: _____

Route: _____ Temp./conditions: _____

Ride time: _____ Total time: _____

Distance: _____ Avg. speed: _____ Max. speed: _____

Fitness: _____ Weight: _____ Pulse: _____

Cross-training: _____

_____

Comments: _____

_____

Weekly Summary

Week of: _____ Week #: _____

Goal hours: _____ Total hours: _____ Goal miles: _____ Total miles: _____

Intensity goal: _____ Avg. speed: _____ Max. speed: _____

Fitness: _____ Weight: _____ Pulse: _____

Other training goals: _____

Cross-training: _____

Equipment/Maintenance: _____

Comments: _____

_____

Monday/Hour:_____ Week of:_____ Week #:_____

Route:_____ Temp./conditions:_____

Ride time:_____ Total time:_____

Distance:_____ Avg. speed:_____ Max. speed:_____

Fitness:_____ Weight:_____ Pulse:_____

Cross-training:_____

Comments:_____

Tuesday/Hour:_____ Week of:_____ Week #:_____

Route:_____ Temp./conditions:_____

Ride time:_____ Total time:_____

Distance:_____ Avg. speed:_____ Max. speed:_____

Fitness:_____ Weight:_____ Pulse:_____

Cross-training:_____

Comments:_____

Wednesday/Hour:_____ Week of:_____ Week #:_____

Route:_____ Temp./conditions:_____

Ride time:_____ Total time:_____

Distance:_____ Avg. speed:_____ Max. speed:_____

Fitness:_____ Weight:_____ Pulse:_____

Cross-training:_____

Comments:_____

Thursday/Hour:_____ Week of:_____ Week #:_____

Route:_____ Temp./conditions:_____

Ride time:_____ Total time:_____

Distance:_____ Avg. speed:_____ Max. speed:_____

Fitness:_____ Weight:_____ Pulse:_____

Cross-training:_____

Comments:_____

Friday/Hour: _____ Week of: _____ Week #: _____

Route: _____ Temp./conditions: _____

Ride time: _____ Total time: _____

Distance: _____ Avg. speed: _____ Max. speed: _____

Fitness: _____ Weight: _____ Pulse: _____

Cross-training: _____

_____

Comments: _____

_____

Saturday/Hour: _____ Week of: _____ Week #: _____

Route: _____ Temp./conditions: _____

Ride time: _____ Total time: _____

Distance: _____ Avg. speed: _____ Max. speed: _____

Fitness: _____ Weight: _____ Pulse: _____

Cross-training: _____

_____

Comments: _____

_____

Sunday/Hour: _____ Week of: _____ Week #: _____

Route: _____ Temp./conditions: _____

Ride time: _____ Total time: _____

Distance: _____ Avg. speed: _____ Max. speed: _____

Fitness: _____ Weight: _____ Pulse: _____

Cross-training: _____

_____

Comments: _____

_____

Weekly Summary

Week of: _____ Week #: _____

Goal hours: _____ Total hours: _____ Goal miles: _____ Total miles: _____

Intensity goal: _____ Avg. speed: _____ Max. speed: _____

Fitness: _____ Weight: _____ Pulse: _____

Other training goals: _____

Cross-training: _____

Equipment/Maintenance: _____

Comments: _____

_____

A man riding a bicycle on the beach; France.

Monday/Hour:_____ Week of: _____ Week #:_____

Route:_____ Temp./conditions:_____

Ride time:_____ Total time: _____

Distance:_____ Avg. speed: _____ Max. speed:_____

Fitness:_____ Weight: _____ Pulse:_____

Cross-training:_____

_____

Comments:_____

_____

Tuesday/Hour:_____ Week of: _____ Week #:_____

Route:_____ Temp./conditions:_____

Ride time:_____ Total time: _____

Distance:_____ Avg. speed: _____ Max. speed:_____

Fitness:_____ Weight: _____ Pulse:_____

Cross-training:_____

_____

Comments:_____

_____

Wednesday/Hour:_____ Week of: _____ Week #:_____

Route:_____ Temp./conditions:_____

Ride time:_____ Total time: _____

Distance:_____ Avg. speed: _____ Max. speed:_____

Fitness:_____ Weight: _____ Pulse:_____

Cross-training:_____

_____

Comments:_____

_____

Thursday/Hour:_____ Week of: _____ Week #:_____

Route:_____ Temp./conditions:_____

Ride time:_____ Total time: _____

Distance:_____ Avg. speed: _____ Max. speed:_____

Fitness:_____ Weight: _____ Pulse:_____

Cross-training:_____

_____

Comments:_____

_____

Friday/Hour:_____ Week of: _____ Week #:_____

Route:_____ Temp./conditions:_____

Ride time:_____ Total time: _____

Distance:_____ Avg. speed: _____ Max. speed:_____

Fitness:_____ Weight: _____ Pulse:_____

Cross-training:_____

Comments:_____

Saturday/Hour:_____ Week of: _____ Week #:_____

Route:_____ Temp./conditions:_____

Ride time:_____ Total time: _____

Distance:_____ Avg. speed: _____ Max. speed:_____

Fitness:_____ Weight: _____ Pulse:_____

Cross-training:_____

Comments:_____

Sunday/Hour:_____ Week of: _____ Week #:_____

Route:_____ Temp./conditions:_____

Ride time:_____ Total time: _____

Distance:_____ Avg. speed: _____ Max. speed:_____

Fitness:_____ Weight: _____ Pulse:_____

Cross-training:_____

Comments:_____

Weekly Summary

Week of:_____ Week #:_____

Goal hours:_____ Total hours: _____ Goal miles: _____ Total miles:_____

Intensity goal: _____ Avg. speed: _____ Max. speed:_____

Fitness:_____ Weight: _____ Pulse:_____

Other training goals:_____

Cross-training: _____

Equipment/Maintenance:_____

Comments:_____

97

TRAINING

Monday/Hour:_____ Week of: _____ Week #:_____

Route:_____ Temp./conditions:_____

Ride time:_____ Total time: _____

Distance:_____ Avg. speed: _____ Max. speed:_____

Fitness:_____ Weight: _____ Pulse:_____

Cross-training:_____

Comments:_____

Tuesday/Hour:_____ Week of: _____ Week #:_____

Route:_____ Temp./conditions:_____

Ride time:_____ Total time: _____

Distance:_____ Avg. speed: _____ Max. speed:_____

Fitness:_____ Weight: _____ Pulse:_____

Cross-training:_____

Comments:_____

Wednesday/Hour:_____ Week of: _____ Week #:_____

Route:_____ Temp./conditions:_____

Ride time:_____ Total time: _____

Distance:_____ Avg. speed: _____ Max. speed:_____

Fitness:_____ Weight: _____ Pulse:_____

Cross-training:_____

Comments:_____

Thursday/Hour:_____ Week of: _____ Week #:_____

Route:_____ Temp./conditions:_____

Ride time:_____ Total time: _____

Distance:_____ Avg. speed: _____ Max. speed:_____

Fitness:_____ Weight: _____ Pulse:_____

Cross-training:_____

Comments:_____

Friday/Hour:_____ Week of: _____ Week #:_____

Route:_____ Temp./conditions:_____

Ride time:_____ Total time: _____

Distance:_____ Avg. speed: _____ Max. speed:_____

Fitness:_____ Weight: _____ Pulse:_____

Cross-training:_____

_____

Comments:_____

_____

Saturday/Hour:_____ Week of: _____ Week #:_____

Route:_____ Temp./conditions:_____

Ride time:_____ Total time: _____

Distance:_____ Avg. speed: _____ Max. speed:_____

Fitness:_____ Weight: _____ Pulse:_____

Cross-training:_____

_____

Comments:_____

_____

Sunday/Hour:_____ Week of: _____ Week #:_____

Route:_____ Temp./conditions:_____

Ride time:_____ Total time: _____

Distance:_____ Avg. speed: _____ Max. speed:_____

Fitness:_____ Weight: _____ Pulse:_____

Cross-training:_____

_____

Comments:_____

_____

Weekly Summary

Week of:_____ Week #:_____

Goal hours:_____ Total hours:_____ Goal miles: _____ Total miles:_____

Intensity goal: _____ Avg. speed: _____ Max. speed:_____

Fitness:_____ Weight: _____ Pulse:_____

Other training goals:_____

Cross-training: _____

Equipment/Maintenance:_____

Comments:_____

_____

Monday/Hour:_____ Week of:_____ Week #:_____

Route:_____ Temp./conditions:_____

Ride time:_____ Total time:_____

Distance:_____ Avg. speed:_____ Max. speed:_____

Fitness:_____ Weight:_____ Pulse:_____

Cross-training:_____

Comments:_____

Tuesday/Hour:_____ Week of:_____ Week #:_____

Route:_____ Temp./conditions:_____

Ride time:_____ Total time:_____

Distance:_____ Avg. speed:_____ Max. speed:_____

Fitness:_____ Weight:_____ Pulse:_____

Cross-training:_____

Comments:_____

Wednesday/Hour:_____ Week of:_____ Week #:_____

Route:_____ Temp./conditions:_____

Ride time:_____ Total time:_____

Distance:_____ Avg. speed:_____ Max. speed:_____

Fitness:_____ Weight:_____ Pulse:_____

Cross-training:_____

Comments:_____

Thursday/Hour:_____ Week of:_____ Week #:_____

Route:_____ Temp./conditions:_____

Ride time:_____ Total time:_____

Distance:_____ Avg. speed:_____ Max. speed:_____

Fitness:_____ Weight:_____ Pulse:_____

Cross-training:_____

Comments:_____

Friday/Hour:_____ Week of:_____ Week #:_____

Route:_____ Temp./conditions:_____

Ride time:_____ Total time:_____

Distance:_____ Avg. speed:_____ Max. speed:_____

Fitness:_____ Weight:_____ Pulse:_____

Cross-training:_____

Comments:_____

Saturday/Hour:_____ Week of:_____ Week #:_____

Route:_____ Temp./conditions:_____

Ride time:_____ Total time:_____

Distance:_____ Avg. speed:_____ Max. speed:_____

Fitness:_____ Weight:_____ Pulse:_____

Cross-training:_____

Comments:_____

Sunday/Hour:_____ Week of:_____ Week #:_____

Route:_____ Temp./conditions:_____

Ride time:_____ Total time:_____

Distance:_____ Avg. speed:_____ Max. speed:_____

Fitness:_____ Weight:_____ Pulse:_____

Cross-training:_____

Comments:_____

Weekly Summary

Week of:_____ Week #:_____

Goal hours:_____ Total hours:_____ Goal miles:_____ Total miles:_____

Intensity goal:_____ Avg. speed:_____ Max. speed:_____

Fitness:_____ Weight:_____ Pulse:_____

Other training goals:_____

Cross-training:_____

Equipment/Maintenance:_____

Comments:_____

TRAINING

Monday/Hour:_____ Week of:_____ Week #:_____

Route:_____ Temp./conditions:_____

Ride time:_____ Total time:_____

Distance:_____ Avg. speed:_____ Max. speed:_____

Fitness:_____ Weight:_____ Pulse:_____

Cross-training:_____

_____

Comments:_____

_____

Tuesday/Hour:_____ Week of:_____ Week #:_____

Route:_____ Temp./conditions:_____

Ride time:_____ Total time:_____

Distance:_____ Avg. speed:_____ Max. speed:_____

Fitness:_____ Weight:_____ Pulse:_____

Cross-training:_____

_____

Comments:_____

_____

Wednesday/Hour:_____ Week of:_____ Week #:_____

Route:_____ Temp./conditions:_____

Ride time:_____ Total time:_____

Distance:_____ Avg. speed:_____ Max. speed:_____

Fitness:_____ Weight:_____ Pulse:_____

Cross-training:_____

_____

Comments:_____

_____

Thursday/Hour:_____ Week of:_____ Week #:_____

Route:_____ Temp./conditions:_____

Ride time:_____ Total time:_____

Distance:_____ Avg. speed:_____ Max. speed:_____

Fitness:_____ Weight:_____ Pulse:_____

Cross-training:_____

_____

Comments:_____

_____

Friday/Hour:_____ Week of:_____ Week #:_____

Route:_____ Temp./conditions:_____

Ride time:_____ Total time:_____

Distance:_____ Avg. speed:_____ Max. speed:_____

Fitness:_____ Weight:_____ Pulse:_____

Cross-training:_____

Comments:_____
_____

Saturday/Hour:_____ Week of:_____ Week #:_____

Route:_____ Temp./conditions:_____

Ride time:_____ Total time:_____

Distance:_____ Avg. speed:_____ Max. speed:_____

Fitness:_____ Weight:_____ Pulse:_____

Cross-training:_____

Comments:_____
_____

Sunday/Hour:_____ Week of:_____ Week #:_____

Route:_____ Temp./conditions:_____

Ride time:_____ Total time:_____

Distance:_____ Avg. speed:_____ Max. speed:_____

Fitness:_____ Weight:_____ Pulse:_____

Cross-training:_____

Comments:_____
_____

Weekly Summary

Week of:_____ Week #:_____

Goal hours:_____ Total hours:_____ Goal miles:_____ Total miles:_____

Intensity goal:_____ Avg. speed:_____ Max. speed:_____

Fitness:_____ Weight:_____ Pulse:_____

Other training goals:_____

Cross-training:_____

Equipment/Maintenance:_____

Comments:_____
_____

Jonathan Page at the Concord Capital Criterium; Concord, New Hampshire.

Monday/Hour:_____ Week of: _____ Week #:_____

Route:_____ Temp./conditions:_____

Ride time:_____ Total time: _____

Distance:_____ Avg. speed: _____ Max. speed:_____

Fitness:_____ Weight: _____ Pulse:_____

Cross-training:_____

Comments:_____

Tuesday/Hour:_____ Week of: _____ Week #:_____

Route:_____ Temp./conditions:_____

Ride time:_____ Total time: _____

Distance:_____ Avg. speed: _____ Max. speed:_____

Fitness:_____ Weight: _____ Pulse:_____

Cross-training:_____

Comments:_____

Wednesday/Hour:_____ Week of: _____ Week #:_____

Route:_____ Temp./conditions:_____

Ride time:_____ Total time: _____

Distance:_____ Avg. speed: _____ Max. speed:_____

Fitness:_____ Weight: _____ Pulse:_____

Cross-training:_____

Comments:_____

Thursday/Hour:_____ Week of: _____ Week #:_____

Route:_____ Temp./conditions:_____

Ride time:_____ Total time: _____

Distance:_____ Avg. speed: _____ Max. speed:_____

Fitness:_____ Weight: _____ Pulse:_____

Cross-training:_____

Comments:_____

TRAINING

Friday/Hour:_____ Week of:_____ Week #:_____

Route:_____ Temp./conditions:_____

Ride time:_____ Total time:_____

Distance:_____ Avg. speed:_____ Max. speed:_____

Fitness:_____ Weight:_____ Pulse:_____

Cross-training:_____

_____

Comments:_____

_____

Saturday/Hour:_____ Week of:_____ Week #:_____

Route:_____ Temp./conditions:_____

Ride time:_____ Total time:_____

Distance:_____ Avg. speed:_____ Max. speed:_____

Fitness:_____ Weight:_____ Pulse:_____

Cross-training:_____

_____

Comments:_____

_____

Sunday/Hour:_____ Week of:_____ Week #:_____

Route:_____ Temp./conditions:_____

Ride time:_____ Total time:_____

Distance:_____ Avg. speed:_____ Max. speed:_____

Fitness:_____ Weight:_____ Pulse:_____

Cross-training:_____

_____

Comments:_____

_____

Weekly Summary

Week of:_____ Week #:_____

Goal hours:_____ Total hours:_____ Goal miles:_____ Total miles:_____

Intensity goal:_____ Avg. speed:_____ Max. speed:_____

Fitness:_____ Weight:_____ Pulse:_____

Other training goals:_____

Cross-training:_____

Equipment/Maintenance:_____

Comments:_____

_____

TRAINING

Monday/Hour:_____ Week of:_____ Week #:_____

Route:_____ Temp./conditions:_____

Ride time:_____ Total time:_____

Distance:_____ Avg. speed:_____ Max. speed:_____

Fitness:_____ Weight:_____ Pulse:_____

Cross-training:_____

Comments:_____

Tuesday/Hour:_____ Week of:_____ Week #:_____

Route:_____ Temp./conditions:_____

Ride time:_____ Total time:_____

Distance:_____ Avg. speed:_____ Max. speed:_____

Fitness:_____ Weight:_____ Pulse:_____

Cross-training:_____

Comments:_____

Wednesday/Hour:_____ Week of:_____ Week #:_____

Route:_____ Temp./conditions:_____

Ride time:_____ Total time:_____

Distance:_____ Avg. speed:_____ Max. speed:_____

Fitness:_____ Weight:_____ Pulse:_____

Cross-training:_____

Comments:_____

Thursday/Hour:_____ Week of:_____ Week #:_____

Route:_____ Temp./conditions:_____

Ride time:_____ Total time:_____

Distance:_____ Avg. speed:_____ Max. speed:_____

Fitness:_____ Weight:_____ Pulse:_____

Cross-training:_____

Comments:_____

TRAINING

Friday/Hour:_____ Week of: _____ Week #:_____
Route:_____ Temp./conditions:_____
Ride time:_____ Total time: _____
Distance:_____ Avg. speed: _____ Max. speed:_____
Fitness:_____ Weight: _____ Pulse:_____
Cross-training:_____
_____
Comments:_____
_____

Saturday/Hour:_____ Week of: _____ Week #:_____
Route:_____ Temp./conditions:_____
Ride time:_____ Total time: _____
Distance:_____ Avg. speed: _____ Max. speed:_____
Fitness:_____ Weight: _____ Pulse:_____
Cross-training:_____
_____
Comments:_____
_____

Sunday/Hour:_____ Week of: _____ Week #:_____
Route:_____ Temp./conditions:_____
Ride time:_____ Total time: _____
Distance:_____ Avg. speed: _____ Max. speed:_____
Fitness:_____ Weight: _____ Pulse:_____
Cross-training:_____
_____
Comments:_____
_____

Weekly Summary

Week of:_____ Week #:_____
Goal hours:_____ Total hours:_____ Goal miles:_____ Total miles:_____
Intensity goal:_____ Avg. speed:_____ Max. speed:_____
Fitness:_____ Weight:_____ Pulse:_____
Other training goals:_____
Cross-training:_____
Equipment/Maintenance:_____
Comments:_____
_____

Monday/Hour:_____ Week of: _____ Week #:_____

Route:_____ Temp./conditions:_____

Ride time:_____ Total time: _____

Distance:_____ Avg. speed: _____ Max. speed:_____

Fitness:_____ Weight: _____ Pulse:_____

Cross-training:_____

Comments:_____

Tuesday/Hour:_____ Week of: _____ Week #:_____

Route:_____ Temp./conditions:_____

Ride time:_____ Total time: _____

Distance:_____ Avg. speed: _____ Max. speed:_____

Fitness:_____ Weight: _____ Pulse:_____

Cross-training:_____

Comments:_____

Wednesday/Hour:_____ Week of: _____ Week #:_____

Route:_____ Temp./conditions:_____

Ride time:_____ Total time: _____

Distance:_____ Avg. speed: _____ Max. speed:_____

Fitness:_____ Weight: _____ Pulse:_____

Cross-training:_____

Comments:_____

Thursday/Hour:_____ Week of: _____ Week #:_____

Route:_____ Temp./conditions:_____

Ride time:_____ Total time: _____

Distance:_____ Avg. speed: _____ Max. speed:_____

Fitness:_____ Weight: _____ Pulse:_____

Cross-training:_____

Comments:_____

Friday/Hour:_____ Week of:_____ Week #:_____

Route:_____ Temp./conditions:_____

Ride time:_____ Total time:_____

Distance:_____ Avg. speed:_____ Max. speed:_____

Fitness:_____ Weight:_____ Pulse:_____

Cross-training:_____

_____

Comments:_____

_____

Saturday/Hour:_____ Week of:_____ Week #:_____

Route:_____ Temp./conditions:_____

Ride time:_____ Total time:_____

Distance:_____ Avg. speed:_____ Max. speed:_____

Fitness:_____ Weight:_____ Pulse:_____

Cross-training:_____

_____

Comments:_____

_____

Sunday/Hour:_____ Week of:_____ Week #:_____

Route:_____ Temp./conditions:_____

Ride time:_____ Total time:_____

Distance:_____ Avg. speed:_____ Max. speed:_____

Fitness:_____ Weight:_____ Pulse:_____

Cross-training:_____

_____

Comments:_____

_____

Weekly Summary

Week of:_____ Week #:_____

Goal hours:_____ Total hours:_____ Goal miles:_____ Total miles:_____

Intensity goal:_____ Avg. speed:_____ Max. speed:_____

Fitness:_____ Weight:_____ Pulse:_____

Other training goals:_____

Cross-training:_____

Equipment/Maintenance:_____

Comments:_____

_____

Monday/Hour:_____ Week of:_____ Week #:_____

Route:_____ Temp./conditions:_____

Ride time:_____ Total time:_____

Distance:_____ Avg. speed:_____ Max. speed:_____

Fitness:_____ Weight:_____ Pulse:_____

Cross-training:_____

_____

Comments:_____

_____

Tuesday/Hour:_____ Week of:_____ Week #:_____

Route:_____ Temp./conditions:_____

Ride time:_____ Total time:_____

Distance:_____ Avg. speed:_____ Max. speed:_____

Fitness:_____ Weight:_____ Pulse:_____

Cross-training:_____

_____

Comments:_____

_____

Wednesday/Hour:_____ Week of:_____ Week #:_____

Route:_____ Temp./conditions:_____

Ride time:_____ Total time:_____

Distance:_____ Avg. speed:_____ Max. speed:_____

Fitness:_____ Weight:_____ Pulse:_____

Cross-training:_____

_____

Comments:_____

_____

Thursday/Hour:_____ Week of:_____ Week #:_____

Route:_____ Temp./conditions:_____

Ride time:_____ Total time:_____

Distance:_____ Avg. speed:_____ Max. speed:_____

Fitness:_____ Weight:_____ Pulse:_____

Cross-training:_____

_____

Comments:_____

_____

Friday/Hour:_____ Week of:_____ Week #:_____

Route:_____ Temp./conditions:_____

Ride time:_____ Total time:_____

Distance:_____ Avg. speed:_____ Max. speed:_____

Fitness:_____ Weight:_____ Pulse:_____

Cross-training:_____

_____

Comments:_____

_____

Saturday/Hour:_____ Week of:_____ Week #:_____

Route:_____ Temp./conditions:_____

Ride time:_____ Total time:_____

Distance:_____ Avg. speed:_____ Max. speed:_____

Fitness:_____ Weight:_____ Pulse:_____

Cross-training:_____

_____

Comments:_____

_____

Sunday/Hour:_____ Week of:_____ Week #:_____

Route:_____ Temp./conditions:_____

Ride time:_____ Total time:_____

Distance:_____ Avg. speed:_____ Max. speed:_____

Fitness:_____ Weight:_____ Pulse:_____

Cross-training:_____

_____

Comments:_____

_____

Weekly Summary

Week of:_____ Week #:_____

Goal hours:_____ Total hours:_____ Goal miles:_____ Total miles:_____

Intensity goal:_____ Avg. speed:_____ Max. speed:_____

Fitness:_____ Weight:_____ Pulse:_____

Other training goals:_____

Cross-training:_____

Equipment/Maintenance:_____

Comments:_____

_____

Bicycle racer; 1897.

Scott Mercier at the Rutland Criterium/Killington Stage Race; Rutland, Vermont.

Monday/Hour:_____ Week of:_____ Week #:_____

Route:_____ Temp./conditions:_____

Ride time:_____ Total time:_____

Distance:_____ Avg. speed:_____ Max. speed:_____

Fitness:_____ Weight:_____ Pulse:_____

Cross-training:_____

_____

Comments:_____

_____

Tuesday/Hour:_____ Week of:_____ Week #:_____

Route:_____ Temp./conditions:_____

Ride time:_____ Total time:_____

Distance:_____ Avg. speed:_____ Max. speed:_____

Fitness:_____ Weight:_____ Pulse:_____

Cross-training:_____

Comments:_____

_____

Wednesday/Hour:_____ Week of:_____ Week #:_____

Route:_____ Temp./conditions:_____

Ride time:_____ Total time:_____

Distance:_____ Avg. speed:_____ Max. speed:_____

Fitness:_____ Weight:_____ Pulse:_____

Cross-training:_____

_____

Comments:_____

_____

Thursday/Hour:_____ Week of:_____ Week #:_____

Route:_____ Temp./conditions:_____

Ride time:_____ Total time:_____

Distance:_____ Avg. speed:_____ Max. speed:_____

Fitness:_____ Weight:_____ Pulse:_____

Cross-training:_____

_____

Comments:_____

_____

Friday/Hour: _____ Week of: _____ Week #: _____

Route: _____ Temp./conditions: _____

Ride time: _____ Total time: _____

Distance: _____ Avg. speed: _____ Max. speed: _____

Fitness: _____ Weight: _____ Pulse: _____

Cross-training: _____

Comments: _____

Saturday/Hour: _____ Week of: _____ Week #: _____

Route: _____ Temp./conditions: _____

Ride time: _____ Total time: _____

Distance: _____ Avg. speed: _____ Max. speed: _____

Fitness: _____ Weight: _____ Pulse: _____

Cross-training: _____

Comments: _____

Sunday/Hour: _____ Week of: _____ Week #: _____

Route: _____ Temp./conditions: _____

Ride time: _____ Total time: _____

Distance: _____ Avg. speed: _____ Max. speed: _____

Fitness: _____ Weight: _____ Pulse: _____

Cross-training: _____

Comments: _____

Weekly Summary

Week of: _____ Week #: _____

Goal hours: _____ Total hours: _____ Goal miles: _____ Total miles: _____

Intensity goal: _____ Avg. speed: _____ Max. speed: _____

Fitness: _____ Weight: _____ Pulse: _____

Other training goals: _____

Cross-training: _____

Equipment/Maintenance: _____

Comments: _____

Monday/Hour:_____ Week of: _____ Week #:_____

Route:_____ Temp./conditions:_____

Ride time:_____ Total time: _____

Distance:_____ Avg. speed: _____ Max. speed:_____

Fitness:_____ Weight: _____ Pulse:_____

Cross-training:_____

Comments:_____

_____

Tuesday/Hour:_____ Week of: _____ Week #:_____

Route:_____ Temp./conditions:_____

Ride time:_____ Total time: _____

Distance:_____ Avg. speed: _____ Max. speed:_____

Fitness:_____ Weight: _____ Pulse:_____

Cross-training:_____

Comments:_____

_____

Wednesday/Hour:_____ Week of: _____ Week #:_____

Route:_____ Temp./conditions:_____

Ride time:_____ Total time: _____

Distance:_____ Avg. speed: _____ Max. speed:_____

Fitness:_____ Weight: _____ Pulse:_____

Cross-training:_____

Comments:_____

_____

Thursday/Hour:_____ Week of: _____ Week #:_____

Route:_____ Temp./conditions:_____

Ride time:_____ Total time: _____

Distance:_____ Avg. speed: _____ Max. speed:_____

Fitness:_____ Weight: _____ Pulse:_____

Cross-training:_____

Comments:_____

_____

TRAINING

TRAINING

Friday/Hour:_____ Week of:_____ Week #:_____
Route:_____ Temp./conditions:_____
Ride time:_____ Total time:_____
Distance:_____ Avg. speed:_____ Max. speed:_____
Fitness:_____ Weight:_____ Pulse:_____
Cross-training:_____
_____
Comments:_____
_____

Saturday/Hour:_____ Week of:_____ Week #:_____
Route:_____ Temp./conditions:_____
Ride time:_____ Total time:_____
Distance:_____ Avg. speed:_____ Max. speed:_____
Fitness:_____ Weight:_____ Pulse:_____
Cross-training:_____
_____
Comments:_____
_____

Sunday/Hour:_____ Week of:_____ Week #:_____
Route:_____ Temp./conditions:_____
Ride time:_____ Total time:_____
Distance:_____ Avg. speed:_____ Max. speed:_____
Fitness:_____ Weight:_____ Pulse:_____
Cross-training:_____
_____
Comments:_____
_____

Weekly Summary

Week of:_____ Week #:_____
Goal hours:_____ Total hours:_____ Goal miles:_____ Total miles:_____
Intensity goal:_____ Avg. speed:_____ Max. speed:_____
Fitness:_____ Weight:_____ Pulse:_____
Other training goals:_____
Cross-training:_____
Equipment/Maintenance:_____
Comments:_____
_____

Monday/Hour:_____ Week of: _____ Week #:_____

Route:_____ Temp./conditions:_____

Ride time: _____ Total time: _____

Distance:_____ Avg. speed: _____ Max. speed:_____

Fitness:_____ Weight: _____ Pulse:_____

Cross-training:_____

Comments:_____

Tuesday/Hour:_____ Week of: _____ Week #:_____

Route:_____ Temp./conditions:_____

Ride time: _____ Total time: _____

Distance:_____ Avg. speed: _____ Max. speed:_____

Fitness:_____ Weight: _____ Pulse:_____

Cross-training:_____

Comments:_____

Wednesday/Hour:_____ Week of: _____ Week #:_____

Route:_____ Temp./conditions:_____

Ride time: _____ Total time: _____

Distance:_____ Avg. speed: _____ Max. speed:_____

Fitness:_____ Weight: _____ Pulse:_____

Cross-training:_____

Comments:_____

Thursday/Hour:_____ Week of: _____ Week #:_____

Route:_____ Temp./conditions:_____

Ride time: _____ Total time: _____

Distance:_____ Avg. speed: _____ Max. speed:_____

Fitness:_____ Weight: _____ Pulse:_____

Cross-training:_____

Comments:_____

Friday/Hour:_____ Week of:_____ Week #:_____

Route:_____ Temp./conditions:_____

Ride time:_____ Total time:_____

Distance:_____ Avg. speed:_____ Max. speed:_____

Fitness:_____ Weight:_____ Pulse:_____

Cross-training:_____
_____

Comments:_____
_____

Saturday/Hour:_____ Week of:_____ Week #:_____

Route:_____ Temp./conditions:_____

Ride time:_____ Total time:_____

Distance:_____ Avg. speed:_____ Max. speed:_____

Fitness:_____ Weight:_____ Pulse:_____

Cross-training:_____
_____

Comments:_____
_____

Sunday/Hour:_____ Week of:_____ Week #:_____

Route:_____ Temp./conditions:_____

Ride time:_____ Total time:_____

Distance:_____ Avg. speed:_____ Max. speed:_____

Fitness:_____ Weight:_____ Pulse:_____

Cross-training:_____
_____

Comments:_____
_____

Weekly Summary

Week of:_____ Week #:_____

Goal hours:_____ Total hours:_____ Goal miles:_____ Total miles:_____

Intensity goal:_____ Avg. speed:_____ Max. speed:_____

Fitness:_____ Weight:_____ Pulse:_____

Other training goals:_____

Cross-training:_____

Equipment/Maintenance:_____

Comments:_____
_____

Monday/Hour:_____ Week of: _____ Week #:_____

Route:_____ Temp./conditions:_____

Ride time:_____ Total time: _____

Distance:_____ Avg. speed: _____ Max. speed:_____

Fitness:_____ Weight: _____ Pulse:_____

Cross-training:_____

Comments:_____

_____

Tuesday/Hour:_____ Week of: _____ Week #:_____

Route:_____ Temp./conditions:_____

Ride time:_____ Total time: _____

Distance:_____ Avg. speed: _____ Max. speed:_____

Fitness:_____ Weight: _____ Pulse:_____

Cross-training:_____

Comments:_____

_____

Wednesday/Hour:_____ Week of: _____ Week #:_____

Route:_____ Temp./conditions:_____

Ride time:_____ Total time: _____

Distance:_____ Avg. speed: _____ Max. speed:_____

Fitness:_____ Weight: _____ Pulse:_____

Cross-training:_____

Comments:_____

_____

Thursday/Hour:_____ Week of: _____ Week #:_____

Route:_____ Temp./conditions:_____

Ride time:_____ Total time: _____

Distance:_____ Avg. speed: _____ Max. speed:_____

Fitness:_____ Weight: _____ Pulse:_____

Cross-training:_____

Comments:_____

_____

121

Friday/Hour:_____ Week of:_____ Week #:_____

Route:_____ Temp./conditions:_____

Ride time:_____ Total time:_____

Distance:_____ Avg. speed:_____ Max. speed:_____

Fitness:_____ Weight:_____ Pulse:_____

Cross-training:_____

_____

Comments:_____

_____

Saturday/Hour:_____ Week of:_____ Week #:_____

Route:_____ Temp./conditions:_____

Ride time:_____ Total time:_____

Distance:_____ Avg. speed:_____ Max. speed:_____

Fitness:_____ Weight:_____ Pulse:_____

Cross-training:_____

Comments:_____

_____

Sunday/Hour:_____ Week of:_____ Week #:_____

Route:_____ Temp./conditions:_____

Ride time:_____ Total time:_____

Distance:_____ Avg. speed:_____ Max. speed:_____

Fitness:_____ Weight:_____ Pulse:_____

Cross-training:_____

_____

Comments:_____

_____

Weekly Summary

Week of:_____ Week #:_____

Goal hours:_____ Total hours:_____ Goal miles:_____ Total miles:_____

Intensity goal:_____ Avg. speed:_____ Max. speed:_____

Fitness:_____ Weight:_____ Pulse:_____

Other training goals:_____

Cross-training:_____

Equipment/Maintenance:_____

Comments:_____

_____

TOURING

Tour de France between Saint-Girons and Cauterets in the Pyrenees mountains.

Date/Hour: _____ Temp./conditions: _____

Participants: _____

Location: _____

Start point: _____ Finish point: _____

Ride time: _____ Total time: _____

Avg. speed: _____ Max. speed: _____

Route: _____ Distance: _____

Points of interest: _____

Comments: _____ Pulse: _____

Date/Hour: _____ Temp./conditions: _____

Participants: _____

Location: _____

Start point: _____ Finish point: _____

Ride time: _____ Total time: _____

Avg. speed: _____ Max. speed: _____

Route: _____ Distance: _____

Points of interest: _____

Comments: _____ Pulse: _____

"It is not enough to know how to do something, you must know why you're doing it." ... in reference to training

—Greg Lemond

Date/Hour: _____ Temp./conditions: _____

Participants: _____

Location: _____

Start point: _____ Finish point: _____

Ride time: _____ Total time: _____

Avg. speed: _____ Max. speed: _____

Route: _____ Distance: _____

Points of interest: _____

Comments: _____ Pulse: _____

Date/Hour: _____ Temp./conditions: _____
Participants: _____
Location: _____
Start point: _____ Finish point: _____
Ride time: _____ Total time: _____
Avg. speed: _____ Max. speed: _____
Route: _____ Distance: _____
Points of interest: _____
Comments: _____ Pulse: _____

"Nothing compares to the simple pleasure of a bike ride."

—John F. Kennedy

TOURING

Date/Hour: _____ Temp./conditions: _____
Participants: _____
Location: _____
Start point: _____ Finish point: _____
Ride time: _____ Total time: _____
Avg. speed: _____ Max. speed: _____
Route: _____ Distance: _____
Points of interest: _____
Comments: _____ Pulse: _____

Date/Hour: _____ Temp./conditions: _____
Participants: _____
Location: _____
Start point: _____ Finish point: _____
Ride time: _____ Total time: _____
Avg. speed: _____ Max. speed: _____
Route: _____ Distance: _____
Points of interest: _____
Comments: _____ Pulse: _____

Chuck Fallon; Southern Utah.

"You're moving through a wonderful natural environment and working on balance, timing, depth perception, judgment...it forms a kind of ballet."

—Charlie Cunningham

Date/Hour: _____ Temp./conditions: _____

Participants: _____

Location: _____

Start point: _____ Finish point: _____

Ride time: _____ Total time: _____

Avg. speed: _____ Max. speed: _____

Route: _____ Distance: _____

Points of interest: _____

Comments: _____ Pulse: _____

Date/Hour: _____ Temp./conditions: _____

Participants: _____

Location: _____

Start point: _____ Finish point: _____

Ride time: _____ Total time: _____

Avg. speed: _____ Max. speed: _____

Route: _____ Distance: _____

Points of interest: _____

Comments: _____ Pulse: _____

Date/Hour: _____ Temp./conditions: _____

Participants: _____

Location: _____

Start point: _____ Finish point: _____

Ride time: _____ Total time: _____

Avg. speed: _____ Max. speed: _____

Route: _____ Distance: _____

Points of interest: _____

Comments: _____ Pulse: _____

"Determination and character. Those are the main qualities for a cyclist."

—Eddy Merckx

Date/Hour: _____ Temp./conditions: _____

Participants: _____

Location: _____

Start point: _____ Finish point: _____

Ride time: _____ Total time: _____

Avg. speed: _____ Max. speed: _____

Route: _____ Distance: _____

Points of interest: _____

Comments: _____ Pulse: _____

Date/Hour: _____ Temp./conditions: _____

Participants: _____

Location: _____

Start point: _____ Finish point: _____

Ride time: _____ Total time: _____

Avg. speed: _____ Max. speed: _____

Route: _____ Distance: _____

Points of interest: _____

Comments: _____ Pulse: _____

Date/Hour: _____ Temp./conditions: _____

Participants: _____

Location: _____

Start point: _____ Finish point: _____

Ride time: _____ Total time: _____

Avg. speed: _____ Max. speed: _____

Route: _____ Distance: _____

Points of interest: _____

Comments: _____ Pulse: _____

Date/Hour: _____ Temp./conditions: _____

Participants: _____

Location: _____

Start point: _____ Finish point: _____

Ride time: _____ Total time: _____

Avg. speed: _____ Max. speed: _____

Route: _____ Distance: _____

Points of interest: _____

Comments: _____ Pulse: _____

Date/Hour: _____ Temp./conditions: _____

Participants: _____

Location: _____

Start point: _____ Finish point: _____

Ride time: _____ Total time: _____

Avg. speed: _____ Max. speed: _____

Route: _____ Distance: _____

Points of interest: _____

Comments: _____ Pulse: _____

Date/Hour: _____ Temp./conditions: _____

Participants: _____

Location: _____

Start point: _____ Finish point: _____

Ride time: _____ Total time: _____

Avg. speed: _____ Max. speed: _____

Route: _____ Distance: _____

Points of interest: _____

Comments: _____ Pulse: _____

"Put me back on my bike."

—**Tommy Simpson;** Reported last words.
Simpson died from heart failure during the Tour de France.

Starting line of BIKE NEW YORK®; 1996.

Date/Hour: _____ Temp./conditions: _____

Participants: _____

Location: _____

Start point: _____ Finish point: _____

Ride time: _____ Total time: _____

Avg. speed: _____ Max. speed: _____

Route: _____ Distance: _____

Points of interest: _____

Comments: _____ Pulse: _____

Date/Hour: _____ Temp./conditions: _____

Participants: _____

Location: _____

Start point: _____ Finish point: _____

Ride time: _____ Total time: _____

Avg. speed: _____ Max. speed: _____

Route: _____ Distance: _____

Points of interest: _____

Comments: _____ Pulse: _____

"We are only as good as our mind, body, and soul in combination. Everything has to be working together in order for you to reach your potential."

—Fred Matheny

Date/Hour: _____ Temp./conditions: _____

Participants: _____

Location: _____

Start point: _____ Finish point: _____

Ride time: _____ Total time: _____

Avg. speed: _____ Max. speed: _____

Route: _____ Distance: _____

Points of interest: _____

Comments: _____ Pulse: _____

"Riders need to learn to be okay with being uncomfortable and understand pain. It's a matter of perception."

—John Brady

Date/Hour: _____ Temp./conditions: _____
Participants: _____
Location: _____
Start point: _____ Finish point: _____
Ride time: _____ Total time: _____
Avg. speed: _____ Max. speed: _____
Route: _____ Distance: _____
Points of interest: _____
Comments: _____ Pulse: _____

Date/Hour: _____ Temp./conditions: _____
Participants: _____
Location: _____
Start point: _____ Finish point: _____
Ride time: _____ Total time: _____
Avg. speed: _____ Max. speed: _____
Route: _____ Distance: _____
Points of interest: _____
Comments: _____ Pulse: _____

Date/Hour: _____ Temp./conditions: _____
Participants: _____
Location: _____
Start point: _____ Finish point: _____
Ride time: _____ Total time: _____
Avg. speed: _____ Max. speed: _____
Route: _____ Distance: _____
Points of interest: _____
Comments: _____ Pulse: _____

RACING

Norm Alvis back in the race after a spill at the Rutland Criterium/Killington Stage Race; Rutland, Vermont.

Date/Hour:_____ Temp./conditions:_____

Event:_____ Location:_____

Partners/team:_____

Category:_____ Course:_____

Distance:_____ Avg. speed:_____

Time/position:_____

Team time/position:_____

Equipment:_____

Comments:_____

_____

Date/Hour:_____ Temp./conditions:_____

Event:_____ Location:_____

Partners/team:_____

Category:_____ Course:_____

Distance:_____ Avg. speed:_____

Time/position:_____

Team time/position:_____

Equipment:_____

Comments:_____

_____

Date/Hour:_____ Temp./conditions:_____

Event:_____ Location:_____

Partners/team:_____

Category:_____ Course:_____

Distance:_____ Avg. speed:_____

Time/position:_____

Team time/position:_____

Equipment:_____

Comments:_____

_____

RACING

"Mountain bikes make you very primitive ... you get to
know the ridges, feel the valleys, suffer over
thousands of feet of climbing and descending."

—Jacquie Phelan

134

Date/Hour:_____ Temp./conditions:_____

Event:_____ Location:_____

Partners/team:_____

Category:_____ Course:_____

Distance:_____ Avg. speed:_____

Time/position:_____

Team time/position:_____

Equipment:_____

Comments:_____

_____

"I see these guys hurting, I see the salt forming on their shorts, I see them sweating, and I'm willing to sacrifice for them."

—Lance Armstrong

Date/Hour:_____ Temp./conditions:_____

Event:_____ Location:_____

Partners/team:_____

Category:_____ Course:_____

Distance:_____ Avg. speed:_____

Time/position:_____

Team time/position:_____

Equipment:_____

Comments:_____

_____

Date/Hour:_____ Temp./conditions:_____

Event:_____ Location:_____

Partners/team:_____

Category:_____ Course:_____

Distance:_____ Avg. speed:_____

Time/position:_____

Team time/position:_____

Equipment:_____

Comments:_____

_____

RACING

In the pack, Bercy sports stadium; Paris, France.

Date/Hour:_____ Temp./conditions:_____

Event:_____ Location:_____

Partners/team:_____

Category:_____ Course:_____

Distance:_____ Avg. speed:_____

Time/position:_____

Team time/position:_____

Equipment:_____

Comments:_____

_____

Date/Hour:_____ Temp./conditions:_____

Event:_____ Location:_____

Partners/team:_____

Category:_____ Course:_____

Distance:_____ Avg. speed:_____

Time/position:_____

Team time/position:_____

Equipment:_____

Comments:_____

_____

Date/Hour:_____ Temp./conditions:_____

Event:_____ Location:_____

Partners/team:_____

Category:_____ Course:_____

Distance:_____ Avg. speed:_____

Time/position:_____

Team time/position:_____

Equipment:_____

Comments:_____

_____

"Treat the race like a time trial. Just go your max."

—Daryl Price

RACING

Date/Hour:_____ Temp./conditions:_____
Event:_____ Location:_____
Partners/team:_____
Category:_____ Course:_____
Distance:_____ Avg. speed:_____
Time/position:_____
Team time/position:_____
Equipment:_____
Comments:_____
_____
_____

"... in cycling, every race you go to is different—the same people, but a different race, and you're always learning."

—Greg Lemond

Date/Hour:_____ Temp./conditions:_____
Event:_____ Location:_____
Partners/team:_____
Category:_____ Course:_____
Distance:_____ Avg. speed:_____
Time/position:_____
Team time/position:_____
Equipment:_____
Comments:_____
_____

Date/Hour:_____ Temp./conditions:_____
Event:_____ Location:_____
Partners/team:_____
Category:_____ Course:_____
Distance:_____ Avg. speed:_____
Time/position:_____
Team time/position:_____
Equipment:_____
Comments:_____
_____

Tim Johnson at Cyclocross; Connecticut.

Date/Hour:_____ Temp./conditions:_____

Event:_____ Location:_____

Partners/team:_____

Category: _____ Course:_____

Distance: _____ Avg. speed:_____

Time/position: _____

Team time/position:_____

Equipment:_____

Comments:_____

_____

Date/Hour:_____ Temp./conditions:_____

Event:_____ Location:_____

Partners/team:_____

Category: _____ Course:_____

Distance: _____ Avg. speed:_____

Time/position: _____

Team time/position:_____

Equipment:_____

Comments:_____

"... the best thing for racing is racing itself, the more you can do, the better."

—Craig Mac Farlane

Date/Hour:_____ Temp./conditions:_____

Event:_____ Location:_____

Partners/team:_____

Category: _____ Course:_____

Distance: _____ Avg. speed:_____

Time/position: _____

Team time/position:_____

Equipment:_____

Comments:_____

Date/Hour:_____ Temp./conditions:_____
Event:_____ Location:_____
Partners/team:_____
Category:_____ Course:_____
Distance:_____ Avg. speed:_____
Time/position:_____
Team time/position:_____
Equipment:_____
Comments:_____

"Each race is ... a test of cunning, cold-bloodedness
and logic, compared by some to playing chess while
driving a formula one racing car at top speed."

—Trip Gabriel

Date/Hour:_____ Temp./conditions:_____
Event:_____ Location:_____
Partners/team:_____
Category:_____ Course:_____
Distance:_____ Avg. speed:_____
Time/position:_____
Team time/position:_____
Equipment:_____
Comments:_____

Date/Hour:_____ Temp./conditions:_____
Event:_____ Location:_____
Partners/team:_____
Category:_____ Course:_____
Distance:_____ Avg. speed:_____
Time/position:_____
Team time/position:_____
Equipment:_____
Comments:_____

RACING

Cathy Marsal pursuing cycling's one-hour speed record; Bordeaux, France; 1995.

CONVERSION TABLE

Kilometers		Miles		Miles		Kilometers	
1 kilometer	=	.62	miles	1	miles	=	1.6	kilometers
5 kilometers	=	3.1	miles	5	miles	=	8	kilometers
10 kilometers	=	6.2	miles	10	miles	=	16	kilometers
15 kilometers	=	9.3	miles	13.1	miles	=	20.96	kilometers
20 kilometers	=	12.4	miles	15	miles	=	24	kilometers
25 kilometers	=	15.5	miles	20	miles	=	32	kilometers
30 kilometers	=	18.6	miles	25	miles	=	40	kilometers
35 kilometers	=	21.7	miles	26.2	miles	=	41.92	kilometers
40 kilometers	=	24.8	miles	30	miles	=	48	kilometers
45 kilometers	=	27.9	miles	35	miles	=	56	kilometers
50 kilometers	=	31	miles	40	miles	=	64	kilometers
55 kilometers	=	34.1	miles	45	miles	=	72	kilometers
60 kilometers	=	37.2	miles	50	miles	=	80	kilometers
65 kilometers	=	40.3	miles	55	miles	=	88	kilometers
70 kilometers	=	43.4	miles	60	miles	=	96	kilometers
75 kilometers	=	46.5	miles	65	miles	=	104	kilometers
80 kilometers	=	49.6	miles	70	miles	=	112	kilometers
85 kilometers	=	52.7	miles	75	miles	=	120	kilometers
90 kilometers	=	55.8	miles	80	miles	=	128	kilometers
95 kilometers	=	58.9	miles	85	miles	=	136	kilometers
100 kilometers	=	62	miles	90	miles	=	144	kilometers
105 kilometers	=	65.1	miles	95	miles	=	152	kilometers
110 kilometers	=	68.2	miles	100	miles	=	160	kilometers
115 kilometers	=	71.3	miles	105	miles	=	168	kilometers
120 kilometers	=	74.4	miles	110	miles	=	176	kilometers
125 kilometers	=	77.5	miles	115	miles	=	184	kilometers
130 kilometers	=	80.6	miles	120	miles	=	192	kilometers
135 kilometers	=	83.7	miles	125	miles	=	200	kilometers
140 kilometers	=	86.8	miles	130	miles	=	208	kilometers
145 kilometers	=	89.9	miles	135	miles	=	216	kilometers
150 kilometers	=	93	miles	140	miles	=	224	kilometers

RACES & TOURS

The following is our editors' selection. For more races and events, contact your local cycling organization (see Cycling Resources, pp. 148–151) or browse relevant web sites (see acknowledgments section; p. 154).

January
First Dozen Ride; Dearborn, Michigan
Cascade Bicycle Club; P.O. Box 31299; Seattle, WA 98103; (206) 522–BIKE
Distance: 53mi

February
Long Beach Criterium Series; Long Beach, California
MTS Cycling Box 3213; Anaheim, CA 92803; (714) 750–9060
Durations: (Pro; 1-3) 80min; (19+ 4, 5; Sr 3; Master 30+ 1-3; Master 40+; Wom 1-3) 50min;
(Master 45+; Wom 4) 45min; (30+ 4, 5; Master 50+) 40min; (Master 55+; Jrs 15-18) 35min; (Jrs 13-14) 25min

March
Allegheny Cycling Assoc. Spring Road Race Series; Georgetown, Pennsylvania
Allegheny Cycling Association; 509B Merchant St.; Ambridge, PA 15003 (412) 266–8481
Distances: (class A) 34mi; (class B) 26mi; (class C) 18mi; (Wom all classes) 18mi

Los Angeles Bike Tour; Los Angeles, California
11110 W. Ohio Ave.; Suite 100; Los Angeles, CA 90025; (310) 444–5544
Distance: 26.2mi

April
Pope Valley Road Race; Napa, California
Napa Valley Velo; St. Helena Cyclery; 1156 Main St.; St. Helena, CA 94574; (707) 963–7736
Distances: 60mi; 40mi

Silver Springs 60; Yorkville, Illinois
Aurora Bicycle Club; P.O. Box 972; Aurora, IL 60507; (630) 892–1010
Distances: 25mi; 45mi; 62mi

Vashon Island Circuit Race; Vashon Island, Washington
Pazzo Velo; 4207 SW Hill St.; Seattle, WA 98116; (206) 932–5921
Distances: (Pro; cat 1, 2) 42mi; (cat 3) 36mi; (Masters A, B; Wom 1, 2, 3) 30mi; (4, 5; Wom cat 4; Jrs 18) 24mi

May
Calvin's 12-Hour Challenge; Springfield, Ohio
Dayton Cycling Club; 351 Somerset Pl.; Waynesville, OH 45068; (513) 897–9104
Distances: 50- and 7-mi loops—as many miles as you can ride in 12hrs

San Luis Rey Cycling Classic; San Luis Rey, California
CELO Pacific Racing Club; P.O. Box 1432; Solana Beach, CA 92075; (619) 942–9103
Distances: 81mi; 58mi; 46mi; 35mi; 23mi; 12mi

Tour de Hunting Park; Philadelphia, Pennsylvania
Team Results Bicycle Club; P.O. Box 34635; Philadelphia, PA 19101; (215) 224–1490
Distances: (Team 1, 2, 3, 4; cat 1, 2, 3) 24mi; (cat 3, 4) 21.6mi; (Masters 35+) 18mi; (Wom) 14.4mi; (cat 5) 9.6mi

June
First State Criterium; Dover, Delaware
FSVS; 818 W. 22nd; Willington, DE 19802; (302) 836–9312
Distances: (cat 1, 2, 3) 32mi; (cat 4; Wom; Vet 30+) 20mi; (cat 5; Wom 4; Vet 40+, 50+) 16mi

Tennessee State Time Trial Championships; Dunlap, Tennessee
8340 Gann Rd.; Soddy Daisy, TN 37379; (423) 842–2554
Distances: (Sr Men & Wom; Masters Men & Wom; Tandem) 40K; (Jr Men) 20K

Tour of Woodbridge; Woodbridge, New Jersey
52 Main St.; Woodbridge, NJ 07095; (908) 636–4040
Distances: (Pro; cat 1, 2) 40mi; (cat 3; Masters 35+, 45+) 20mi; (Wom) 15mi; (cat 4, 5) 10mi

July
1st Capital Cycling Classic Criterium; York, Pennsylvania
1st Capital Velo Club; 2857 Sparrow Dr.; York, PA 17404; (717) 792–4400
Distances: (cat 2, 3) 50K; (cat 4, 5) 35K; (Jrs; Masters 30+, 40+, 50+; Wom) 20K; (Public) 10K

Firecracker 100 Bicycle Tour; Brighton, Michigan
Michigan Council AYH; 3024 Coolidge Rd.; Berkley, MI 48072; (248) 545–0511
Distances: 15mi; 25mi; 50mi; 100mi

Harvard Classic; Harvard, Massachusetts
Northeast Bicycle Club, Inc.; 39 Marion Rd.; #2; Belmont, MA 02178; (617) 484–7204
Distances: (cat 1, 2, 3) 100K; (Wom cat 3) 53K; (cat 5; Wom cat 4; Tandem) 33K; (Jr 15-18 yrs) 20K; (Jr 10-14 yrs) 7K

San Pedro Grand Prix; San Pedro, California
Back on Track; P.O. Box 10111; Torrance, CA 90505; (310) 318–2277
Distances: 32mi; 28mi; 20mi; 19.2mi; 16.8mi; 15.2mi; 12.8mi

August
The American Randonnee; Newton, Massachusetts
Boston-Montreal-Boston; Jennifer Weiss; 42 Greenwood Dr.; Bluffton, SC 29910; (803) 757–4191
Distance: 750mi (1200K)

Future Champions Cycling Club Fitness Park Criterium; Trexlertown, Pennsylvania
1605 Cardinal Dr.; Bethlehem, PA 18015; (610) 966–5486
Distances: (cat 1, 2) 30mi; (cat 3) 26mi; (cat 4) 22mi; (cat 5) 18mi; (Jr Men & Wom) 12mi

Hotter 'N Hell Hundred; Witchita Falls, Texas
P.O. Box 2099; Witchita Falls, TX 76307; (940) 723–5800
Distances: 100mi; 100K; 50mi; 10K

Suburban Cable Bicycle Race; Pottstown, Pennsylvania
64 Bethel Church Rd.; Spring City, PA 19475; (610) 495–5644
Distances: (cat 2, 3) 21mi; (cat 3, 4, 5; Masters 30+) 18mi; (Masters 40+; Wom) 14mi; (Tandem) 10mi

September
Harbor Springs Cycling Classic; Harbor Springs, Michigan
Birchwood Inn; 7077 Lake Shore Dr.; Harbor Springs, MI 49740; (800) 530–9955
Distances: 20mi; 40mi; 100K

North Shore Century; Evanston, Illinois
Evanston Bicycle Club; P.O. Box 1981; Evanston, IL 60204; (847) 866–7743
Distances: 100mi; 62mi; 50mi; 25mi

October
Blue Water Ramble; St. Clair, Michigan
Blue Water Ramble; P.O. Box 1435; Sterling Hgts., MI 48311; (810) 468–6605
Distances: 40mi; 60mi; 80mi; 100mi

FCCC Turkey Chase; Trexlertown, Pennsylvania
Clinton River Riders; P.O. Box 1435; Sterling Hgts., MI 48311; (810) 468–6605
Distances: 40mi; 60mi; 80mi; 100mi

TRIATHLONS & DUATHLONS

March

Athens Triathlon; Athens, Texas
Henderson County YMCA; 14 Loyola Dr.; Athens, TX 75751; (903) 675–9154
Distances: 300m S; 12mi B; 5K R

Tucson Triathlon; Tucson, Arizona
3323 N. Honeycomb Ct.; Tucson, AZ 85750; (520) 885–7996
Distances: 825 yd S; 12mi B; 3mi R

April

St. Anthony's Triathlon-Ironman Qualifier; St. Petersburg, Florida
Box 12588; St. Petersburg, FL 33733; (813) 825–1271
Distances: 0.9mi S; 24.8mi B; 6.2mi R

YMCA Strutters Duathlon-Long Race; San Angelo, Texas
305 S Randolph; San Angelo, TX 76903; (817) 355–1279
Distances: 10K R; 60K B; 10K R

May

Fuji Biathlon and Triathlon; Crystal City, Virginia
Triathlantic Association; P.O. Box 28477; Baltimore, MD 21234; (410) 882–6103
Distances: (Biathlon) 5K R; 30K B; 5K R; (Triathlon) 1.5K S; 40K B; 10K R

Greenwich Point Biathlon; Greenwich, Connecticut
Threads & Treads; 17 E. Putman Ave.; Greenwich, CT 06830; (203) 661–0142
Distances: 2.5mi R; 10mi B; 2.5mi R

Island Beach Duathlon; So. Seaside Park, New Jersey
LIN-MARK Computer Sports; 7 Westwood Dr.; Mantua, NJ 08051; (609) 468–0010
Distances: 2.5mi R; 17mi B; 2.5mi R

June

Alcatraz Triathlon; San Francisco, California
ENVIRO-SPORTS; P.O. Box 1040; Stinson Beach, CA 94970; (415) 868–1829
Distances: 1.5mi S (warm-up); 2mi R; 18mi B; 10mi R

Cambridge Endurance Triathlon; Cambridge, Maryland
Columbia Triathlon Association; 6662 Windsor Ct.; Columbia, MD 21044; (410) 964–1246
Distances: 1.2mi S; 13.1mi R; 56mi B

New York State Duathlon; Beaver Island State Park, Grand Island, New York
P.O. Box 225; Grimsby, Ontario, Canada, L3M 4G3; (905) 945–6608; fax (905) 945–8592
Distances: 3K R; 24K B; 3K R

Women's Classic Triathlon; Forest Grove, Oregon
AA Sports, Ltd.; 4840 SW Western Ave.; Suite 400; Beaverton, OR 97005; (503) 644–6822
Distances: 0.5mi S; 11mi B; 5K R

July

Desert Sun Half Iron Triathlon; Highline Lake State Park-Grand Junction, Colorado
Sports Connection; 1062 Main St.; Grand Junction, CO 81501; (970) 241–6786; fax (970) 243–6455
Distances: 1.2mi S; 56mi B; 13.1mi R

Great Catskill-Half Ironman; Kingston, New York
LIN-MARK Computer Sports; 7 Westwood Dr.; Mantua, NJ 08051; (609) 468–0010
Distances: 1.2mi S; 56mi B; 13.1mi R

Powerman Sky Duathlon-Zofingen Qualifier, Powerman Jr. Sky Duathlon; Evergreen, Colorado
Box 4524; Boulder, CO 80306; (303) 652–0399
Distances: 2mi R; 40mi B; 11mi R or 2mi R; 20mi B; 4mi R

Triathlantic Triathlon Series; Lewisberry, Pennsylvania
Triathlantic Association; P.O. Box 28477; Baltimore, MD 21234; (410) 882–6103
Distances: .75mi S; 17.6mi B; 3mi R

August
Fairmount Park Classic Triathlon; Philadelphia, Pennsylvania
Pennsylvania Triathlon Club; P.O. Box 21332; Lehigh Valley, PA 18002; (610) 437–6237
Distances: .9mi S; 23mi B; 6.2mi R

Massachusetts Triathlon; Sharon, Massachusetts
Time Out! Productions; P.O. Box 543; Forestdale, MA 02644; (508) 477–6311
Distances: 0.5mi S; 12mi B; 4.4mi R

Mike & Rob's Most Excellent Triathlon; Ventura State Beach, California
Columbia Triathlon Association; 6662 Windsor Ct.; Columbia, MD 21044; (410) 964–1246
Distances: (long course) 1.2mi S; 56mi B; 13.1mi R; (short course) .25mi S; 9mi B; 3mi R

New England Triathlon Festival; Sunappe, New Hampshire
Time Out! Productions; Box 543; Forestdale, MA 02644; (508)477–6311
Distances: 1mi S; 44mi B; 9mi R

Triathlantic Biathlon Series; Cambridge, Maryland
Triathlantic Association; P.O. Box 28477; Baltimore, MD 21234; (410) 882–6103
Distances: 3mi R; 20mi B; 3mi R

September
Cascades Edge Duathlon; Molalla, Oregon
AA Sports, Ltd.; 4840 SW Western Ave.; Suite 400; Beaverton, OR 97005; (503) 644–6822
Distances: 10K R; 31K B

Skylands Triathlon; Clinton, New Jersey
LIN-MARK Computer Sports; 7 Westwood Dr.; Mantua, NJ 08051; (609) 468–0010
Distances: 0.5mi S; 14.3mi B; 5K R

YMCA Fall Triathlon; Fredericksburg, Virginia
212 Butler Rd.; Falmouth, VA 22405; (540) 371–9622; fax (540) 899–3694
Distances: 15K B; 500meter S; 3.5mi R

October
Tyler's Duathlon and 5K Run; Cincinnati, Ohio
Health and Fitness Promotions; 2029 Riverside Dr.; Suite 102; Columbus, OH 43221; (614) 487–1916
Distances: 5K R; 30K B; 5K R or 5K Run event

Great Floridian Triathlon; Clermont, Florida
CFT/Summer Sports; P.O. Box 121236; Clermont, FL 34712; (352) 394–1320
Distances: 2.4mi S; 112mi B; 26.2mi R

November
Ultraman; Kailua Kona, Hawaii
Ultraman; 78-7170 Ha'awina St.; Kailua-Kona, HI 96740; (808) 322–2120; fax (808) 322–3553;
Distances: 6.2mi S; 90mi B; 171.4mi B; 52.4mi R

Mid-Atlantic

Annapolis Bicycle Club; *P.O. Box 224; Annapolis, MD 21404; (410) 721–9151*

Baltimore Bicycle Club; *P.O. Box 5894; Baltimore, MD 21282; (410) 792–8308*

Bicycle Federation of America; *1506 21st St. NW; Suite 200; Washington, D.C. 20036; (202) 463–6622*

The Bicycle Network; *P.O. Box 8194; Philadelphia, PA 19101; (215) 222–1253*

Bicycle Touring Club of North Jersey; *P.O. Box 839; Mahwah, NJ 07430; (201) 284–0404*

League of American Bicyclists; *190 W. Ostend St.; Suite 120; Baltimore, MD 21230; (410) 539–3399*

Lehigh Valley Velodrome; *217 Main St.; Emmaus, PA 18049; (610) 967–7587*

Nelson Bicycle Alliance; *9994 Rockfish Valley; Afton, VA 22920; (540) 456–6746*

Pennsylvania Bicycle Club; *609 Montgomery Rd.; Ambler, PA 19002; (215) 542–7181*

Quaker City Wheelmen; *1026 Serpentine Ln.; Wyncote, PA 19095; (215) 886–4828*

South Mountain Velo Club; *600 Brenton St.; Shippensburg, PA 17257 (717) 530–1422*

Team Snow Valley; *912 Monroe St.; Annapolis, MD 21403; (410) 721–8990*

United States Bicycling Hall of Fame; *166 W. Main St.; Somerville, NJ 08876; (800) 242–9253*

Washington Area Bicyclist Assoc.; *818 Conn. Ave.; Suite 300; Washington, D.C. 20006; (202) 872–9830*

White Clay Bicycle Club; *1104 Monteray Pl.; Wilmington, DE 19809; (302) 764–1803*

Midwest/Plains

Bike Burlington, Inc.; *P.O. Box 1136; Burlington, IA 52601; (319) 754–4410*

Central Indiana Bicycling Association; *P.O. Box 55405; Indianapolis, IN 46205; (317) 327–2453*

Chicagoland Bicycle Federation; *417 S. Dearborn; Room 1000; Chicago, IL 60605; (312) 427–3325*

Cycling Saddlemen Bicycle Club; *1547 Dowling; Westland, MI 48186; (313) 278–1350*

League of Illinois Bicyclists; *417 S. Dearborn; Room 1000; Chicago, IL 60605; (708) 481–3429*

League of Michigan Bicyclists; *P.O. Box 16201; Lansing, MI 04890; (517) 394–2453*

Major Taylor Velodrome; *3649 Cold Spring Rd.; Indianapolis, IN 46222; (317) 327–8356*

Maple City Bicycling Club; *P.O. Box 55; La Porte, IN 46352; (219) 362–4200*

Mid-America Bicycle Club; *2216 Central Ave.; Kearney, NE 68847; (308) 234–3822*

National Bicycle League; *3958 Brown Park Dr.; Suite D; Hilliard, OH 43026; (800) 886–2691*

Ohio Bicycle Federation; *825 Olde Farm Court; Vandalia, OH 45377; (513) 890–6689*

Springbike Bicycle Club; *P.O. Box 10013; Springfield, MO 65808; (417) 886–8901*

Spring City Spinners; *P.O. Box 2055; Waukesha, WI 53186; (414) 297–9135*

Team Columbus; *6124 Freeman Rd.; Westerville, OH 43082; (614) 890–4145*

Twin Cities Bicycle Club; *P.O. Box 131086; Roseville, MN 55113; (612) 924–2443*

Velo Ventures; *7115 W. North Ave.; Oak Park, IL 60302; (708) 848–9524*

Northeast/New England

Bicycle Coalition of Massachusetts; *214A Broadway; Cambridge, MA 02142; (617) 495–7408*

BIKE NEW YORK®; *891 Amsterdam Ave; New York, NY 10025; (212) 932–2300 ext. 243*

Central Connecticut Cycling; *P.O. Box 310973; Newington, CT 06131; (860) 667–0380*

Granite State Wheelmen; *2 Townsend Ave.; Salem, NH 03079; (603) 898–5479*

Maine Wheels Bicycle Club; *225 Paris Hill Rd.; South Paris, ME 04281; (207) 743–2577*

National Cycle League International; *532 Laguardia Pl.; New York, NY 10012; (212) 777–3611*

New York Cycle Club; *P.O. Box 1343; Midtown Station; New York, NY 10018; (212) 886–4545*

Northeast Bicycle Club, Inc.; *39 Marion Rd.; #2; Belmont, MA 02178; (617) 484–7204*

Zephyr Cycling Team; *129 Mill St.; Naugatuck, CT 06770; (203) 723–8182*

South

Austin Cycling Association; *P.O. Box 5993; Austin, TX 78763; (512) 477–0776*

The Baton Rouge Velodrome; *701 Jefferson Hwy.; Jefferson, LA 70121; (504) 837–3600*

Blue Ridge Bicycle Club; *P.O. Box 304; Asheville, NC 28802; (704) 684–1085*

Brian Piccolo Park Velodrome; *9501 Sheridan St.; Cooper City, FL 33024; (954) 437–2600*

Carolina Cyclers; *P.O. Box 11163; Columbia, SC 29211; (803) 783–0698*

Coastal Valley Cycling Association; *P.O. Box 14531; Savannah, GA 31416; (912) 898–0020*

East Point Velodrome; *1513 East Cleveland Ave.; Suite 301-B; East Point, GA 30344; (404) 209–5146*

Gainesville Cycling Club; *5015 NW 19th Pl.; Gainesville, FL 32605; (352) 378–7063*

Houston Bike Club; *P.O. Box 52752; Houston, TX 77052; (713) 935–2810*

Louisville Wheelmen; *P.O. Box 35541; Louisville, KY 40232; (502) 329–1848*

Mid-Cities Wheelmen Road Racing Team; *836 Birdsong Dr.; Bedford, TX 76021; (817) 282–7958*

Montgomery Bicycle Club; *P.O. Box 231116; Montgomery, AL 36123; (334) 365–9728*

Nashville Bicycle Club; *P.O. Box 158593; Nashville, TN 37215; (615) 352–8301*

New Orleans Bicycle Club; *P.O. Box 55115; Metairie, LA 70055; (504) 866–6640*

San Antonio Bicycle Racing Club; *1819 Eagle Meadow; San Antonio, TX 78248; (210) 493–5878*

Southern Cyclists; *P.O. Box 2554; Statesboro, GA 30459; (912) 764–7047*

Team Florida; *1005-B SW 3rd Ave.; Gainesville, FL 32601; (352) 377–0245*

Texas Bicycle Coalition; *P.O. Box 1121; Austin, TX 78767; (512) 476–7433*

Ultra Marathon Cycling Association; *P.O. Box 53; Canyon, TX 79015; (806) 499–3210*

Southwest/Rockies

Adventure Cycling Association; *P.O. Box 8308; Missoula, MT 59807; (406) 721–1776*

American Bicycle Association; *9831 S. 51st St.; Suite D135; Phoenix, AZ 85044; (602) 961–1903*

Arizona Bicycle Club; *P.O. Box 7191; Phoenix, AZ 85011; (602) 254–9572*

Bicycle Racing Association of Colorado; *4615 E. 23rd Ave.; Denver, CO 80207; (303) 440–5366*

Bicycle Utah; *P.O. Box 738; Park City, UT 84060; (801) 649–5806*

BikeCentennial; *P.O. Box 8308; Missoula, MT 59801; (406) 721–1776*

Cycling Utah; *P.O. Box 57980; Salt Lake City, UT 84157; (801) 268–2652*

Denver Bicycle Touring Club; *P.O. Box 101301; Denver, CO 80250; (303) 756–7240*

International Mountain Bicycling Association; *P.O. Box 7578; Boulder, CO 80306; (303) 545–9011*

National Off-Road Bicycling Association; *One Olympic Plaza; Colorado Springs, CO 80909; (719) 578–4717*

Pikes Peak Mountain Bike Club; *7001 White Buffalo Rd.; Colorado Springs, CO 80919; (719)522–0574*

Red Robin Bicycle Tour of CO; *3500 South Wadsworth Blvd.; Ste. 201; Lakewood, CO 80235; (800) 985–9399*

Triathlon Federation/USA; *P.O. Box 15820; Colorado Springs, CO 80935; (719) 597–9090*

Twin Rivers Cyclists, Inc.; *P.O. Box 2108; Lewiston, ID 83501; (509) 758–3919*

United States Cycling Federation; *One Olympic Plaza; Colorado Springs, CO 80909; (719) 578–4581*

West

AA Sports Limited; *4840 SW Western Ave.; Suite 400; Beaverton, OR 97005; (503) 644–6822*

California Association of Bicycling Organizations; *P.O. Box 2684; Dublin, CA 94568; (310) 639–9348*

California Bicycle Coalition; *909 12th St.; Suite 100; Sacramento, CA 95814; (916) 446–7558*

Cascade Bicycle Club; *P.O. Box 31299; Seattle, WA 98103; (206) 522–2453*

Hawaii Bicycling League; *P.O. Box 4403; Honolulu, HI 96812; (808) 735–5756*

Hellyer Velodrome; *Northern CA Velodrome Assoc.; 985 Hellyer Ave.; San Jose, CA 95111; (510) 531–1400*

Juneau Freewheelers Bicycle Club; *P.O. Box 34475; Juneau, AK 99801; (907) 463–3095*

Los Angeles Bike Tour; *1110 W. Ohio Ave.; Los Angeles, CA 90025; (310) 444–5544*

Marymoor Velodrome Association; *6218 29th Ave. NE; Seattle, WA 98115; (206) 389–5825*

Salem Bicycle Club; *P.O. Box 2224; Salem, OR 97308; (503) 588–8613*

San Diego Velodrome Association; *2221 Morley Field Dr.; San Diego, CA 92019; (619) 296–3345*

San Francisco Bicycle Coalition; *1095 Market St.; Suite 215; San Francisco, CA 94103; (415) 431–2453*

PERSONAL CONTACTS

Name:_____ Phone:_____
Address:_____
Days/times available to train:_____

Name:_____ Phone:_____
Address:_____
Days/times available to train:_____

Name:_____ Phone:_____
Address:_____
Days/times available to train:_____

Name:_____ Phone:_____
Address:_____
Days/times available to train:_____

Name:_____ Phone:_____
Address:_____
Days/times available to train:_____

Name:_____ Phone:_____
Address:_____
Days/times available to train:_____

Name:_____ Phone:_____
Address:_____
Days/times available to train:_____

Name:_____ Phone:_____
Address:_____
Days/times available to train:_____

Name:_____ Phone:_____
Address:_____
Days/times available to train:_____

Name:_____ Phone:_____
Address:_____
Days/times available to train:_____

MAINTENANCE CALENDAR

January _____

_____

_____

_____

February _____

_____

_____

_____

March _____

_____

_____

_____

April _____

_____

_____

_____

May _____

_____

_____

_____

June _____

_____

_____

_____

MAINTENANCE CALENDAR

July

_____

_____

_____

_____

August

_____

_____

_____

September

_____

_____

_____

October

_____

_____

_____

_____

November

_____

_____

_____

December

_____

_____

_____

_____

ACKNOWLEDGMENTS

We would like to thank Liz Barrett and Bruce Messite for their time and valuable input, without which this book would not have been possible; Thanks to the photographers—Jonathan McElvery and Jack Popowich; and to the Photography Stock Agencies—AP/Wide World Photos, BIKE NEW YORK®, Nancy Marshall and the Maine Office of Tourism, Magnum Photos, Inc., SIPA Press, and UPI/Corbis-Bettmann, for use of their photos. Thanks also to all the websites which were a valuable source of information: Northern California Bicycle Racing (http://www-graphics.stanford.edu/~cck/racing.html), New Jersey Online Biking (http://www.nj.com/bike/racing/racelink.html), Cycling org...the global cycling network (http://cycling.org/), The League of American Bicyclists (http://www.bikeleague.org/), North American Bicycle Racing Calendar (http://www.TrueSport.com/Bike/cycling.htm), The Bicycle Exchange (http://www.bikexchange.com/index.htm), Cool Running (http://www.coolrunning.com), VeloNews interactive (http://www.velonews.com), Triathlete Online (http://www.triathletemag.com), The Triathlete's Web (http://w3.one.net/~triweb/triweb.html), Super Jock 'N Jill (http://www.jock-n-jill.com/sjj/welcome.html), Web Runner Running Page (http://www-webrunner.com/webrun/running/running.html).

Special thanks to Neil Ortenberg, Matt Trokenheim, and Daniel O'Connor at Thunder's Mouth Press for their enthusiastic support of this project.

PHOTO CREDITS

pp. i, 14 courtesy of AP/Wide World Photos
pp. ii, 136 © Martine Franck; Magnum Photos, Inc.
pp. v, vi, 5, 32, 41, 50, 77, 104, 114, 133, 139 © Jonathan McElvery
pp. 23, 59, 68, 95, 113 courtesy of UPI/Corbis-Bettmann
p. 86 © David Boe; UPI/Corbis-Bettmann
p. 95 © Magnum Photos, Inc.
p. 123 © Laurent Rebours; AP/Wide World Photos
p. 126 © Jack Popowich
p. 130 courtesy Dave Trattles; BIKE NEW YORK®
p. 142 courtesy SIPA Press